SCOTUS and COVID

SCOTUS and COVID

How the Media Reacted to the Livestreaming of Supreme Court Oral Arguments

Rachael B. Houston, Timothy R. Johnson, and Eve M. Ringsmuth

ROWMAN & LITTLEFIELD
Lanham • Boulder • New York • London

Published by Rowman & Littlefield
An imprint of The Rowman & Littlefield Publishing Group, Inc.
4501 Forbes Boulevard, Suite 200, Lanham, Maryland 20706
www.rowman.com

86-90 Paul Street, London EC2A 4NE

British Library Cataloguing in Publication Information Available

Library of Congress Cataloging-in-Publication Data Available

ISBN 9781538172612 (cloth) | ISBN 9781538172629 (paper) |
ISBN 9781538172636 (epub)

♾™ The paper used in this publication meets the minimum requirements of American National Standard for Information Sciences—Permanence of Paper for Printed Library Materials, ANSI/NISO Z39.48-1992.

For the best family I could ever ask for: Stephen, Nolan, and Nathaniel. —RBH

This one is for the boys: Alexi Matthew, Aidan Marshall, and Satchel Henry. —TRJ

For my unfailingly supportive, and always encouraging, mom, Marybeth. —EMR

Contents

List of Figures ix

List of Tables xi

Acknowledgments xiii

Introduction: The Supreme Court, Media Coverage,
and Oral Arguments 1

1 Examining News Media Coverage of Supreme Court
   Oral Arguments 17

2 Did Livestreamed Arguments Increase Online Print Media
   Coverage of Supreme Court Oral Arguments? 33

3 Did Livestreamed Arguments Change How Online Print
   Media Covered the Court? 47

4 Did Livestreamed Arguments Change the Volume and
   Content of Broadcast Media Coverage? 69

Conclusion 87

Appendix: Variable Codebook and Additional Tables and Models 95

Bibliography 107

Notes 115

Index 127

About the Authors 133

Figures

Figure 1.1 Press Release from US Supreme Court Public
Information Office Announcing Livestreamed Arguments   19
Figure 1.2 What C-SPAN Livestreaming Viewers Saw on May 4,
2020 When Justice Stephen Breyer and Attorney Lisa
Blatt Interacted during Oral Arguments in *U.S. Patent
& Trademark Office v. Booking.com* (2020)   20
Figure 2.1 Average Number of Online Print Media Stories about
Orally Argued Cases (2019–2021 Terms)   36
Figure 2.2 Number of Online Print Media Oral Argument Stories
by Ideological Leaning of News Outlets (2019–2021
Terms)   40
Figure 2.3 Probability That an Online Print News Story Was
Published about an Orally Argued Case (2019–2021
Terms)   44
Figure 3.1 Average Word Count of Online Print News Stories
about Orally Argued Cases (2019–2021 Terms)   51
Figure 3.2 Average Number of Times Online Print Media Outlets
Quote Justices (2019–2021 Terms)   53
Figure 3.3a Number of Individual Justice Quotes Used by Online
and 3.3b Print Media Outlets (2019–2021 Terms)   54
Figure 3.4 Number of Attorney Quotes Used by Online Print
Media Outlets (2019–2021 Terms)   57
Figure 3.5 Percentage of Justice or Advocate Quotes That Are at
Least One Full Sentence in Online Print News Stories
(2019–2021 Terms)   59

Figure 3.6   Percentage of Online Print Media Stories That Are Original (2019–2021 Terms)   62

Figure 3.7   Number of Online Print Media Stories with at Least One Embedded Audio Clip (2019–2021 Terms)   63

Figure 3.8   Probability That an Online Print News Story Contains at Least One Justice Quote (2019–2021 Terms)   67

Figure 4.1   Number of Broadcast News Stories about Orally Argued Cases (2019–2021 Terms)   71

Figure 4.2   Number of Broadcast News Stories about Orally Argued Cases by Ideological Leanings of News Outlets   74

Figure 4.3   Word Cloud of Top Fifty Words Used in Broadcast News Transcripts about Orally Argued Cases before Livestreaming Began (2019 Term)   83

Figure 4.4   Word Cloud of Top Fifty Words Used in Broadcast News Transcripts about Orally Argued Cases during First Month of Livestreaming (2019 Term)   84

Figure 4.5   Word Cloud of Top Fifty Words Used in Broadcast News Transcripts about Orally Argued Cases during the 2020 and 2021 Terms   85

Tables

Table 1.1   Media Outlets Included in Oral Argument Media Coverage Dataset   22

Table 1.2   Ideological Leanings of News Outlets Included in Oral Argument Media Coverage Dataset   23

Table 1.3   Percentage of Stories in the Dataset Produced about Orally Argued Cases by Each Online Print News Outlet (2019–2021 Terms)   25

Table 1.4   Percentage of Stories in the Dataset Produced about Orally Argued Cases by Each Broadcast News Outlet (2019–2021 Terms)   29

Table 2.1   Top Twenty-Five Most Covered Orally Argued Cases by Online Print Media Outlets (2019–2021 Terms)   38

Table 2.2   Logistic Regression of Whether Online Print News Stories Published a Story About an Orally Argued Case (2019–2021 Terms)   43

Table 3.1   Top Twenty-Five Cases with the Most Justice Quotes in Online Print News Stories (2019–2021 Terms)   56

Table 3.2   Percentage of Justice or Advocate Quotes That Are at Least One Full Sentence in Online Print News Stories (2019–2021 Terms)   60

Table 3.3   Logistic Regression of Whether Online Print News Stories Include at Least One Justice Quotation from an Orally Argued Case (2019–2021 Terms)   66

Table 4.1   Number of Broadcast News Stories about Supreme Court Orally Argued Cases (2019–2021 Terms)   72

Table 4.2 Top Ten Most Covered Orally Argued Cases by
Broadcast Media (2019–2021 Terms) 78

Table A Logistic Regression of Whether Online Print News
Stories Published a Story About an Orally Argued
Case (2019–2021 Terms) with May 2020 Session as
Reference Category 104

Table B Logistic Regression of Whether Online Print News
Stories Published a Story About an Orally Argued Case
(2019–2021 Terms), Excluding May 2020 Session 104

Table C Logistic Regression of Whether Online Print News
Stories Include at Least One Justice Quotation from an
Orally Argued Case (2019–2021 Terms) with May 2020
Session as Reference Category 105

Table D Logistic Regression of Whether Online Print News
Stories Include at Least One Justice Quotation from
an Orally Argued Case (2019–2021 Terms), Excluding
May 2020 Session 105

Acknowledgments

This book began, as many academic books do, as an idea just bandied about over coffee between colleagues. Houston was working on her dissertation about public opinion, the Supreme Court, and social media at the same time Ringsmuth and Johnson were focused on how COVID-19 changed the dynamics of justices' behavior during US Supreme Court oral arguments. Houston raised the possibility of analyzing how media covered the change in argument procedure. Not to let an amazing idea go to waste, we gathered some initial data and presented them in a paper at the 2021 Midwest Political Science Association meeting. We were not sure what to do because we had so much data and multiple hypotheses to test—essentially too much for a single paper. When Becca Beurer contacted us about the possibility of turning the paper into a book, we jumped. So, we threefold expanded our database and wrote this book concentrating on whether the media increased coverage when the Court began to livestream its arguments as well as on how the nature of their coverage changed. This book is the culmination of that effort, and there are many people we need to thank.

The book could not, and would not, have been written without the assistance and encouragement of Becca Beurer and her staff at Roman and Littlefield. Becca's guidance as an editor has been first rate, and we could not have completed this project without her excellent help!

During the data collection, research, and writing processes, many people provided us with great help and insight. Specifically, we owe a debt of gratitude to Kjersten Nelson, Jessica Schoenherr, Mike Nelson, Matt Hitt, Sara Benesh, and the participants on our 2021 Midwest Political Science Association Annual meeting panel where the paper that led to the book was first presented publicly.

Houston thanks her absolute best friend and husband Stephen Earnest. She appreciates all the support, love, and food and beer outings that made the

xiv Acknowledgments

writing of this book possible. Houston also thanks Nolan and Nathaniel, who were born, started crawling, and now are about to start walking, all while this book was being written. The boys clearly did not want mom to ever work on this book but at least they have a new bedtime story, and a long one at that! Houston has unyielding gratitude for the Department of Political Science at Texas Christian University. Her colleagues are the greatest, and she could not be more grateful for their support during the writing of this book. Finally, Houston is indebted to her amazing coauthors, Eve Ringsmuth and Tim Johnson, who made this book such a fun project on which to work.

Ringsmuth thanks Simon Ringsmuth for his unconditional love and support. She is grateful for his patience, positivity, and humor, and for the knowledge that they are always on the same team. Ringsmuth thanks Isaac and Jonah for their love and help in keeping her priorities straight. She would also like to thank family and friends for their encouragement, especially Marybeth and Maurice Champion-Garthe, John and Heather Van Sice, John and Sue Ringsmuth, Dani Alderman, Andrea Adams, Sarah Prior, Beth Ringsmuth Stolpman, Ian Van Sice, Sean Van Sice, Wendi Ringsmuth, Peter and Kristena Rudloff, Kjersten Nelson, Logan Dancey, and the one and only Lee 0/1 Bears. Finally, Ringsmuth is so grateful for her two incredibly skilled and insightful coauthors, Rachael Houston and Tim Johnson.

Johnson thanks his partner in crime, Julie Maynard-Johnson, who has kept him grounded every single day for more than thirty years. His writing is better because of her, and she is a master at trying to ensure he always thinks before he speaks. Beyond his immediate family, Johnson is also immensely grateful for the scores of undergraduates and graduate students who have worked with him throughout the past quarter century. He is particularly grateful for Ryan C. Black, Amanda Savage, Sarah Treul, Justin Wedeking, Maron Sorenson, Siyu Li, Tom Pryor, Paul Snell, Charles Gregory, Vincent Vecera, Dion Farganis, Matthew Roberts, and Isaiah Ogren. Finally, he is incredibly thankful that Eve Ringsmuth and Rachael Houston persuaded him to join in this endeavor. He is forever grateful!

We gratefully acknowledge the work of the many research assistants who collected data for us. All three of us fundamentally believe that working with undergraduates (and particularly first-generation students and students of color) is a key part of our love of teaching. Students certainly learn a lot in the classroom but the hands-on experience of being a research assistant takes students into what it really means to be a social scientist. So, we are delighted that we could work with so many amazing colleagues who have the same love of law, politics, and social sciences as do we. In no particular order, we thank Alec Williams, Cadley Schafer, Ian Metzger, Isaiah Ogren, Khalid Mahamud, James Cook, Jazmine Velasquez, Josie Brody, Lauren Simpson, Samantha Woodward, Grace Hertzog, Suhail A. Rizvi, and Taylor Hvidsten.

Introduction

The Supreme Court, Media Coverage, and Oral Arguments

In May 2020, two unprecedented events occurred at the US Supreme Court. For the first time in its history, the justices held oral arguments remotely (via telephone) and, perhaps more importantly, they allowed media outlets and the public at large to listen to these proceedings in real time from anywhere in the world.[1] They made these changes because the COVID-19 pandemic rendered it impossible for justices, counsel, and spectators to meet in open court.[2] While Chief Justice John Roberts and the associate justices thought livestreaming arguments would be a short-term fix, the Court has continued to do so to this day. Indeed, although the justices returned to in-person arguments in October 2021, they still livestreamed audio from their proceedings since the Court remained closed to the public "out of concern for the health and safety of the public and Supreme Court employees."[3] And on September 28, 2022, the Court issued a press release confirming its intent to continue livestreaming during the October 2022 Term, allowing the world to continue to listen and learn even while 50 to 100 people are lucky enough to, once again, gain physical access to courtroom seats.[4]

The pandemic-induced changes to the Court's oral argument protocols were certainly an extraordinary shift away from its long-standing traditions of meeting in person and prohibiting those in attendance—including reporters—from using electronic devices of any kind (e.g., cameras, cell phones, or laptops) to record the proceedings (Schubert et al. 1992; Wasby et al. 1976; Carter 2012). Indeed, while the Court has recorded the audio of its argument sessions since 1955, it was not until 1993 that it began to release the audio files—for media and public consumption—instead of sending them to the National Archives and Records Administration (NARA).[5] Even then (with rare exceptions), the Court did not release the audio until the beginning of the next term—well after most Americans had forgotten about most cases.[6] It was not until the beginning of the 2010 Term that the Court released audio, after the conference, at the end of each argument week.[7] More recently, it has released audio the same day a case is heard but, still, usually hours after the proceedings take place.[8] Thus, until May of 2020, the audio held limited usefulness for timely media reporting of what transpired during oral argument proceedings.

By livestreaming the audio, the Court significantly expanded access to the public and news media alike. We are interested in the degree to which this instantaneous access altered how news media outlets covered the Court's oral arguments and, by extension, the flow of information presented to the public about the Supreme Court. In particular, we seek to examine how this newfound access altered the *volume and nature of coverage*.[9]

This is an especially important issue because the specialized legal language used to discuss cases during oral argument (and in the Court's written opinions), combined with limited access to the courtroom itself, makes it impractical for most individuals to learn directly from the Court about its proceedings and decisions. Instead, the public relies on news coverage, which is created, written about, aired, or streamed, at the discretion of media outlets. In turn, variation in how the news media present information about the Court is the conduit through which individuals shape their views of its rulings (e.g., Wedeking and Zilis 2022; Zilis 2015; Linos and Twist 2016; Hitt and Searles 2018; Slotnick and Segal 1998) and, ultimately, make decisions about its institutional legitimacy (e.g., Caldeira and Gibson 1992; Gibson and Caldeira 2009; Johnston and Bartels 2010).

Given the integral role the news media play in connecting the public and the Court, *we examine the extent to which livestreamed audio changed news media coverage of the Supreme Court*. To make this assessment, we employ a variety of lenses through which we compare the volume and nature of coverage from major mainstream media outlets from all oral argument sessions in the October 2019, October 2020, and October 2021 Terms, accounting for twenty sessions.[10] More specifically, this provides us with 48 cases argued in person before livestreaming began, 66 cases argued via telephone with livestreaming, and 60 cases argued in person with livestreaming. As our interest lies in how the media covered and potentially adapted its coverage, we gathered 926 online print and broadcast news stories produced about oral argument during our terms of interest.

Using these data that we lay out more fully in chapter 1, we demonstrate that livestreaming of oral argument sessions dramatically increased the frequency of news media coverage initially, at least for online print media. Similarly, online print news stories were longer (based on word count), used more direct quotes from the proceedings, and invoked longer quotes from the justices during the first livestreamed argument sessions held in May of

2020. However, these changes in news media coverage did not persist as the Court continued livestreaming during its October 2020 and October 2021 Terms. While online print coverage diverged from broadcast media coverage in the short term, our analysis shows that for both types of outlets, access to livestreamed oral argument audio did not lead to significant long-term changes in coverage.

SIGNIFICANCE OF THE BOOK

These general findings make three major contributions to the scholarly understanding of the Supreme Court's relationship with the media and the public. First, they provide timely evidence that speaks to the current and ongoing debate about public access to the US Supreme Court. While the Court has not committed, long term, to livestreaming oral arguments, it faces increasing pressure, from a variety of institutions, to continue this practice in perpetuity.[11] For instance, American Bar Association president Judy Perry Martinez wrote a public letter asking the Court to continue to livestream audio, citing the "increased transparency, accountability, and opportunity to improve [the public's] understanding of the vital role of the Supreme Court in [individuals'] daily lives" (Robert 2020). Members of the Supreme Court Bar agreed and, in March 2022, sent a similar letter to Roberts imploring him to continue the practice of livestreaming.[12] Additionally, there have been other calls for increased access to the Court. For example, in 2019 Senators Chuck Grassley (R-IA) and Patrick Leahy (D-VT), both former chairs of the Senate Judiciary Committee, jointly penned a letter calling for cameras in the courtroom (Golde 2020b).[13]

In terms of the public, one poll indicates 83 percent of Americans support a continuation of live audio (Golde 2020a) and major media outlets, including *The Washington Post*, report that "The [audio] broadcasts have been an unmitigated success" (Editorial Board 2020). Our conclusion outlines the likely consequences of permanently continuing the livestreaming of oral argument audio and sheds light on the ramifications of other potential expansions in access to the Court, including video coverage of the argument sessions (see, e.g., Black et al. 2022).

Second, our findings speak, more broadly, to the impact on individuals of increased access to the inner workings of government institutions. Indeed, the US Supreme Court is not the only institution to grapple with the constraints of the COVID-19 pandemic and opportunities for unprecedented, and instantaneous, access to anyone, anywhere in the world.[14] Better understanding the results of the Court's decision to livestream audio from its proceedings provides leverage on the consequences of greater government access for news media coverage and, by extension, individuals' exposure to, and interaction with, all levels of government from city councils to school boards, to state legislative committee proceedings and beyond.

Third, we speak to the cross-disciplinary literature that focuses on institutions and institutional change. By institutions we mean, generally, the formal or informal rules that structure interactions between political or social actors (Knight 1992; North 1990). For our phenomenon of interest, we speak to the rules that structure media access to the Court, mainly through oral argument proceedings. Further, when such rules change, as they did at several phases of the COVID-19 pandemic, scholarship demonstrates actors learn and adapt their behavior to such vicissitudes (see, e.g., North 1990; Knight 1992; March and Olsen 1996; Johnson 2004; Dovers and Hezri 2010; Ringsmuth et al. 2023). In the context of the Court, we focus on how the media altered its coverage when the Court moved to livestreamed argument, how it changed again when the Court continued this practice, and, finally, how it reacted when the Court moved to in-person, with simultaneous livestreamed, arguments. By demonstrating the ability of institutions and political actors to adapt to changing rules and circumstances, we bring systematic data to a widely accepted theory that has been largely tested with anecdotal evidence (but see, e.g., Black et al. 2013).

In making these contributions, we use the remainder of this introduction to build our theoretical argument around the confluence of several literatures. First, because our focus is on how the media cover Supreme Court oral argument, we begin with the relationship between news media, the public, and the Court and why we expect the media to initially react to the rule change but then to adapt as the Court chose to retain this practice across (at least) two more terms. We then turn to a history of access to the Court—for the media and individuals alike. Third, we discuss why access to the Court's arguments is vitally important because of the degree to which they affect the justices' decision-making process. Combined, we then posit these literatures suggest the media would alter how it covered the Court's oral arguments audio and why we expect that such an effect would not be a permanent one. After laying out this argument, we provide a chapter outline of the book.

THE TRADITIONAL RELATIONSHIP BETWEEN THE MEDIA, INDIVIDUALS, AND THE COURT

The Court, despite shying away from the media, depends on coverage more than the elected branches of government (Johnson and Socker 2012; LaRowe and Hoekstra 2014). While the elected branches are held accountable to the public through elections, the Court is not. This means the public must show its support for the Court by believing it is a legitimate institution. In other words, the public must support the Court or else the justices' decisions may not be enforced or taken seriously. Many scholars have studied factors that influence public support for the institution, including exposure to the Court and knowledge gained about it (Gibson and Caldeira 2009; Gibson, Caldeira, and Spence 2003). The media certainly influence people's support for the Court in both ways: it can expose the public to the Court and provide key insights into the decisions the justices make.

However, compared to the other branches of government, the Court is not as frequently covered by print media and television (Hoekstra 2003; Slotnick and Segal 1998). This is at least in part because the justices rarely attempt to communicate directly with journalists about their decisions, personal lives, and what it means to be a justice.[15] Journalists feel this lack of communication from the Court as well. As Steve Bensen (MSNBC) put it, "the Court is set in its old ways, and justices feel quite comfortable ignoring outside pressure for change since they don't really answer to anyone."[16]

Without direct communication between journalists and the Court (and even clear opposition, at times, to such communication), journalists either previously had to secure one of the limited in-person seats for the press at oral argument, wait until the recording of the argument was put online at the end of the week, or read through lengthy transcripts to report on what was said during the proceedings. These tasks can be extremely time consuming, especially if journalists are under tight deadlines.

And yet, most individuals come to understand the Court and its decisions *nearly entirely* through this limited news media environment (Leighley 2004; Davis 1994; Davis and Strickler 2000). In other words, the small number of seats available in the courtroom (Peters 2013) and the technical nature of judicial opinions combine to make news media reporting the primary mechanism through which the public learns about the Supreme Court's consideration of cases and decisions.[17] Such coverage of the Court fills a key gap for the public by providing timely information in a format more digestible and accessible to them. Without media reporting on the Court, the public would only be able to learn about it through reading lengthy opinions or listening to hour(s)-long oral arguments. This heavy reliance on the news media, combined with a lack of access to the Court, has meant the public is generally less knowledgeable about it compared to the elected branches (Davis 1994; Davis and Strickler 2000; Haltom and Cadwallader 1998; Slotnick and Segal 1998).

THE DIFFICULTY OF COVERING
THE US SUPREME COURT

Despite the intermediary role served by the news media, the Court's long-standing policies regarding media access clash with the twenty-four-hour news cycle that drives contemporary reporting.[18] Indeed, media coverage in the twenty-first century is dominated by increasingly quick cycles with new stories and details every twenty-four hours or fewer (Vasterman 2005). For Ritter (2020), such advances change what people perceive as relevant and salient news. As he put it, "technological advances in the last part of the twentieth century may have set into motion a catalytic reformation of the relationship . . . between media and the public" (Ritter 2020, 244). Beyond this general finding, scholars have explored myriad ways in which media set the agenda for what news is considered salient in such a frenetic environment (see, e.g., Conway et al. 2015; Harder et al. 2017; Vargo et al. 2018; Vonbun et al. 2016).

However, two aspects of the Court's policies regarding access contrast with the demands and pace of the twenty-first-century news cycle. First, the Court still moves, for the most part, at the speed of its unofficial mascot: the turtle (Lithwick and West 2014). Hitt and Searles put it more bluntly: "A defining feature of political media in the 21st century is the 24-hour television news cycle. In stark relief stands the United States Supreme Court's decidedly more 19th century approach: Print copies of the decision are distributed" (Hitt and Searles 2018, 566). This almost exclusive focus on opinions (see, e.g., Spill and Oxley 2003; Slotnick and Segal 1998) is not generally conducive to the quick and continuously updated media coverage associated with the contemporary news cycle. That is, except for end-of-term cases being handed down within days of one another, opinions come out at a very slow pace throughout the course of a term (see, e.g., Epstein et al. 2014).

Second, the only other public aspect of the Court's process and our phenomenon of interest here—oral arguments—is not widely accessible to the media, making timely reporting more challenging. Space in the courtroom is extremely limited. Thirty-six seats are reserved for members of the press (Howe 2020), meaning that only a select few reporters are permitted to attend the Court's proceedings in person.[19] Further, electronic devices are not allowed in the courtroom (Hitt and Searles 2018). This means that many reporters cannot personally attend while the Court also controls access to the audio and transcripts of the argument proceedings. The former is only released at the end of each argument week, which effectively ends the news cycle (even for salient cases) quite quickly, because any compelling audio soundbites would be days old by the time they are available. As for the latter, even the written transcripts come out at the end of each argument day, which means the news cycle may have already peaked, changed, or even ended prior to their dissemination.

The bottom line is that the Court's norms do not fit well with the generally quick news cycle that exists for almost all other topics covered by the media. As Hitt and Searles sum up, "This media 'strategy' highlights a tension between news media and the Court: Court communications are ill-suited to the modern media environment" (2018, 566). In the next section, we lay out why this is the case for our phenomenon of interest—coverage of oral arguments.

(LIMITED) PUBLIC ACCESS TO SUPREME COURT ORAL ARGUMENT

The federal government puts on many impressive displays in Washington, DC. Every four years the nation celebrates the inauguration of a new president and hundreds of thousands of people attend.[20] Once a year, during a president's term in office, Congress invites them to give an appraisal of the state of the union in front of all senators and representatives, the cabinet, some (sometimes all) Supreme Court justices, and various other dignitaries. Any day Congress is in session, visitors may obtain passes to sit in the Senate or House galleries to watch the legislative process in action. People may also watch extensive coverage of both houses on various C-SPAN channels or online streams. What each of these events has in common is that thousands, hundreds of thousands, or even millions of people can and do witness them. In other words, it is relatively easy for citizens to see their elected representatives in action– whether watching in person, on television, or through various streaming outlets.

In contrast, the pinnacle of the third branch of government—the US Supreme Court—is not in the public eye as often as is Congress or the president. There are at least three factors that contribute to this outcome. First, as we point out above, the courtroom has limited available seating. Even those who are lucky enough to witness an oral argument usually only glimpse about three minutes of the give-and-take between attorneys and the justices. But if you are willing to stand in line for several hours, it is well worth the wait. Of course, in highly salient cases the lines can be extraordinarily long, and the Court anticipates when this may happen. For example, in *Planned Parenthood of Southeastern Pennsylvania v. Casey* (1992) the Court's public information officer, Toni House, sent a memo detailing seating arrangements for the gallery. Among other factors, only 100 seats were reserved for the public and the line for those seats was officially formed at midnight on the day of the argument session (Johnson and Goldman 2009).

And what citizens miss if they are not in the courtroom is nothing short of spectacular. Indeed, the US Supreme Court normally sits for oral arguments between the first Monday in October and the last week in April.[21] At precisely 10 o'clock on argument days, the justices enter the courtroom through the red velvet curtains behind the bench. After other business is finished (e.g., orders issued and new members of the bar sworn in), the chief justice calls the first case and the petitioner's attorney moves to the lectern and begins their argument with the ubiquitous, "Mr. Chief Justice and may it please the Court." These procedures have been status quo for at least as long as the Court has recorded its oral arguments, beginning in the 1955 Term.[22] They encapsulate the stability and normalcy of the nation's highest Court.

Like almost every other aspect of American life, the stability and normalcy of argument sessions were disrupted in early 2020 by the COVID-19 pandemic. Three press releases demonstrate how the justices dealt with this, potentially dire, situation. First, on March 16th the Court said that

> In keeping with public health precautions recommended in response to COVID-19, the Supreme Court is postponing the oral arguments currently scheduled for the March session (March 23-25 and March 30-April 1). The Court will examine the options for rescheduling those cases in due course in light of the developing circumstances.[23]

Second, on April 28th the justices canceled the remaining April sessions and moved to remote arguments:

> The Court will hear oral arguments by telephone conference on May 4, 5, 6, 11, 12 and 13 in a limited number of previously postponed cases. In keeping with public health guidance in response to COVID-19, the Justices and counsel will all participate remotely.[24]

On April 30th the Court issued a final announcement before beginning its telephonic experiment:

> The Court will provide a live audio feed of the arguments to FOX News (the network pool chair), the Associated Press, and C-SPAN, and they will in turn provide a simultaneous feed for the oral arguments to livestream on various media platforms.[25]

Further, the Court simply hears very few cases. While as late as 1992 the justices sat for more than 100 cases per term, today that number averages fewer than seventy per term.[26] This means the justices are largely inaccessible to most individuals, even those who make the trek to Washington, DC, to experience government in action. Finally, the Court does not provide video (livestreamed or delayed) coverage of its oral arguments or opinion announcements in the same way Congress or executive agencies provide such footage of their proceedings and decision-making processes.[27] Thus, even if people want to see the Court in action, beyond the audio and written transcripts of the proceedings, they have very limited opportunity to do so.

Certainly, the move to telephonic arguments was a major change but, for us, the Court's more important concession was to allow the public at large to listen in real time to the justices' sparring with attorneys. Indeed, for the first time, the public and media would enjoy instantaneous access to the justices' questions and comments, as well as to the attorneys' responses to them, in all argued cases.[28] To understand why it was so astonishing, we next offer a brief history of the Court's reticence to allow public access, beyond attending in person, to its argument proceedings.

EVOLVING ACCESS TO SUPREME COURT ORAL ARGUMENTS

While the Court began recording its public sessions in 1955, the reel-to-reel tapes on which it did so were sent only to the NARA for cataloging. Certainly, they were still technically available to individuals, the media, and Court scholars, but they were not exactly accessible—at least easily. Indeed, if a researcher wanted to use the audio files, they would contact the Archives and then NARA would make copies for use by research archivists who would physically pick up the copies or have copies mailed to them. This process often took several months and most cases were clearly no longer salient by that point in time—particularly for the purposes of press coverage.

It took almost forty years for the next change when, in 1993, the Court altered its rules to make the audio slightly more publicly accessible. However, the tapes were released to the media only at the end of each Court term—oftentimes up to a year after an argument took place. So, while access again seemed to increase, the audio was still essentially an historical record rather than an immediate, newsworthy, account of the sessions. In other words, for our purposes, it did not offer additional help for media coverage.

The next incremental change came less than a decade later. In December 2000, the Court began making certain cases more available to the public and media.[29] At the behest of Chief Justice William H. Rehnquist, the audio of oral arguments could be released on the day of the proceedings if heightened public interest warranted such an expedited release.[30] These were not simultaneous (i.e., live) feeds from the courtroom, however. Rather, they were delayed releases that occurred within a few hours of the arguments. Despite this policy, Rehnquist, and eventually Roberts, took this action in only a handful of cases including *Bush v. Gore* (2000), *Hamdi v. Rumsfeld*

(2004), *Rumsfeld v. Padilla* (2004), *Boumediene v. Bush* (2008), *Al Odah v. United States* (2008), *Baze v. Rees* (2008), *NFIB v. Sebelius* (2012), *Obergefell v. Hodges* (2015), and *Trump v. Hawaii* (2018). The point is that the Court sometimes released same day audio but only when the justices believed a case was particularly salient. In other words, this was a slightly better policy for media access but still far from ideal.[31]

In a move toward fuller access, the Court opened its 2006 Term with another procedural shift. Although the rule governing audio release at the beginning of the term proceeding did not change, the justices began to release written argument transcripts the same day cases were heard.[32] Yet, like the previous changes, the release was still not immediate. Rather, it was delayed to the extent that the transcripts came out at the end of each argument day. For media coverage (our phenomenon of interest) this was still a flawed solution because media deadlines often passed before the full transcripts were available and thus, importantly, the twenty-four-hour news cycle in which the case was most salient had usually ended as well.

Four years later, beginning with the October 2010 Term, the Court upped the ante. While it continued to release transcripts the same day cases were argued, it also decided to release the full audio of arguments on its supremecourt.gov website at the end of each argument week.[33] This decision was hailed by Court watchers as another step toward full access while others were not so sure.[34] For our purposes, this change in procedure still did not help media outlets because at least two twenty-four-hour news cycles (or three or four) would pass before reporters could actually listen to what transpired— unless, of course, they were present for a particular argument session.[35]

The Court significantly increased access in May of 2020 (during its October 2019 Term), not because the justices wanted to do so, but out of necessity. As we elaborated above, it was the COVID-19 pandemic that led the justices to livestream audio of their oral arguments precisely because nobody from the public or the press could attend the proceedings. The question to which we next turn is why this is so important. The answer is that oral arguments provide great insight into how and why justices decide the way they do.

WHY ACCESS TO SUPREME COURT ORAL ARGUMENT AUDIO IS VITAL

Supreme Court oral argument is an integral part of the justices' decision-making process. For every case, the justices receive a substantial amount of information through litigant and *amicus curiae* (friend of the Court) briefs. These briefs inform the Court about the legal merits of various arguments and the policy and strategic implications of potential outcomes. Briefs are very important to how the justices decide, and the evidence of their usefulness is clear (Collins 2007; Corley 2008; Schoenherr and Black 2019). However, the justices passively receive this information—they do not directly control what the parties include in their briefs.

Oral argument is different: here the justices actively seek out information that they deem relevant to their decision-making (Johnson 2001, 2004; Ringsmuth and Johnson 2013). Specifically, they use oral argument to resolve factual ambiguities, to consider the merits of various arguments, and to assess the policy implications of their potential rulings (see, e.g., Johnson 2004; Rehnquist 1984). As Justice John M. Harlan described, "There is no substitute . . . for the Socratic method of procedure in getting at the real heart of an issue and in finding out where the truth lies" (Harlan 1955, 7).

While some Supreme Court decisions may appear inevitable, empirical studies suggest advocate quality and experience in oral argument influence how justices vote (see, e.g., Johnson et al. 2006). More experienced attorneys may be more persuasive, at least in part, because they are better able to reduce the costs that justices must pay when obtaining information. In other words, good advocates can facilitate the justices' goal to use oral argument to gather information (for a broad overview of this argument see Johnson (2004).

In addition to gathering information, previous research indicates that justices use oral arguments as a window into their colleagues' perspectives on a case (Black et al. 2012; Sullivan and Canty 2015). Indeed, during these proceedings, they learn about each other's preferences (Johnson 2004; Black et al. 2012), they try to shape each other's view of a case (Black et al. 2012), and they engage in preliminary negotiations about the final decision (Wasby et al. 1976; Black et al. 2012). This forward-looking role is apparent from the archival papers of Justices Lewis F. Powell and Harry A. Blackmun, which indicate that those two justices listened to their colleagues' comments with an ear toward assessing how coalitions might form and particularly how their colleagues might vote (Johnson 2004; Black et al. 2012). Comments from the justices over the years also support this function of oral argument. For example, Justice Anthony Kennedy noted that "[During oral arguments] the Court is having a conversation with itself through the intermediary of the attorney."[36] Additionally, Justice Antonin Scalia commented, "It isn't just an interchange between—between counsel and each of the individual Justices . . . What is going on is also to some extent an exchange of information among the Justices themselves."[37]

Even justices on the current Court discuss how their collegial interactions during these proceedings help them determine what may happen at later stages of their decision-making process. Roberts has noted, "[W]hen we get on the bench it's really the first time we get some clues about what our colleagues think. So we often are using questions to bring out points that we think our colleagues ought to know about."[38] Justice Sonia Sotomayor described one purpose of oral argument "is for judges to hear what's bothering each other" and that "she tailors her own reasoning [during conference] to take account of what she has heard from her colleagues at arguments" (Liptak 2011). Justice Elena Kagan reinforced this view: "There's no doubt . . . that part of what oral argument is about is a little bit of the justices talking to each other with some helpless person standing at the podium who you're talking through" (Liptak 2013). The justices also step in during oral argument when they think the argument is proceeding down the wrong path, hoping to keep their colleagues focused on the issues they deem most likely to produce the "correct" outcome (Johnson 2004; Jacobi and Sag 2019). As such, oral argument has long been an important part of the Court's process that plays a direct role in providing information to the justices and an indirect role in shaping the decision-making of the Court as a whole, enabling the justices to influence one another and form coalitions.

Scholars and court watchers have also used the oral arguments to predict case outcomes and individual justices' votes (see, e.g., Johnson et al. 2009; Black et al. 2011). Specific behaviors justices exhibit during these proceedings are particularly pertinent to making such predictions. For instance, several studies show justices speak more to the party they ultimately vote against (see, e.g., Johnson et al. 2009). This result holds whether it is based on word counts, speech turns, the emotional nature of the justices' questions, and even based on comments that adduce laughter from the gallery (Shullman 2004; Roberts 2005; Black et al. 2011; Jacobi and Sag 2019; Li and Prior 2020).

Furthermore, studies demonstrate that the interactions between justices during oral argument, based on their behavior toward one another, affect behavior in later parts of their decision-making process. For example, inter-justice conflict at oral argument, in the form of interruptions, predicts future breakdowns in voting agreement (Black et al. 2012). In addition, when justices do interrupt one another there is likely to be retribution (the interrupted becomes the interrupter later in the argument) which leads to conflicts between these justices during the opinion writing process (Black et al. 2012). For the foregoing reasons, it is clear that oral arguments, and the ability to listen to them, are vitally important precisely because they are so important to how the justices decide.

Scholars have also shown that justices are influenced by the broader political environment, including public opinion (see, e.g., Bryan 2020; Bryan and Kromphardt 2016). Indeed, public esteem for the Court as an institution is vital since the Court lacks the ability to carry out its decisions (Gibson et al. 2003). Oral argument is central to the Court's legitimacy as an institution because it is the only public portion of the decision-making process.[39] Indeed, justices select cases (Perry 1994), hold conference discussions (Black and

Johnson 2019), and write and bargain over how to craft opinions (Maltzman et al. 2000; Wahlbeck et al. 1998) in private.[40] Public access to oral argument therefore provides a vital opportunity for the public to see the Court impartially exploring questions of national significance through a balanced adjudicative process (Jacobi and Sag 2019), exhibiting the democratic values of equality, transparency, and fairness.

The key takeaways from this literature are that oral argument plays an integral role in how US Supreme Court justices make decisions and is central to the Court's legitimacy. Thus, changes in access to oral argument and how these proceedings are portrayed in the media have broad institutional significance. In the next section, we turn to how the media dealt with this change in access, in the form of livestreaming, to oral argument. To do so, we begin with a discussion of how political actors and institutions adapt to rule changes.

WHY WE EXPECT THE MEDIA TO ADAPT TO CHANGES IN ORAL ARGUMENT ACCESS

Institutions are the formal or informal rules that structure interactions between social actors (Knight 1992; North 1990). Further, when rules and norms change, existing scholarship demonstrates social and political actors respond by adapting their behavior (see, e.g., North 1990; Knight 1992; March and Olsen 1996; Johnson 2004; Dovers and Hezri 2010). In the general context of the Court's relationship to the media, institutions may constrain the media insofar as the rules of the game may prevent them from always covering arguments in the timeliest manner possible because access to the audio or written transcripts of the argument sessions have been made available at various times since the justices began recording their sessions in 1955. While we argue that the media should exhibit a dramatic increase in coverage in response to instant access to oral argument audio, scholars consistently demonstrate political actors can and do adapt to institutions when rules and norms change (see, e.g., North 1990; Knight 1992; March and Olsen 1996; Johnson 2004; Dovers and Hezri 2010). The Court's continuation of its livestreaming policy in the 2020 and 2021 Terms allows us to examine whether the media adapted after their initial immediate access to the argument audio.

In contrast to the Court's longstanding norms, the availability of live streamed oral argument audio notably increased access to these proceedings. The question that piques our interest is how might such availability have changed the way the news media covered the Supreme Court, specifically the volume and nature of coverage? To answer this query, we begin by focusing on why we would expect access to livestreaming to change the *volume* of news coverage. For this, we turn to the literature that examines calculations made by media outlets regarding what to cover and how to do so. According to Livingston and Bennett's (2003) conception of the gatekeeping model, there are four different "gates" that affect the construction of news content. The fourth gate is the most applicable for our purposes. It includes "information and communication technologies that define the limits of time and space in news gathering" (368). Technology that helps reduce the time that content is delivered, and therefore impacts its immediacy, can shape what news outlets decide to cover. In our case, livestreaming was a new technology for the Court that reduced the time for gathering information about oral arguments—and tore down the technology gate of the gatekeeping model. Media outlets could report on information about the Court immediately, which may have been a consideration for them when deciding on what to cover and how to do so.

Other communications literature reinforces the role immediacy plays in determining what to cover. In fact, as speed becomes an inalienable element of journalistic culture, scholars dub modern journalism as "McJournalism" (Franklin 2005) or "McNews" (Rosenberg and Feldman 2008). People want to be informed about relevant changes in their world as soon as possible (Drok and Hermans 2016). Journalists see this fast dissemination of news as their most important task when determining what stories to cover (Weaver and Willnat 2012).

However, the fast-paced nature of journalism means that journalists have to constantly be on their toes—moving from one big news story to the next to keep up with relevant changes in the world.[41] Even covered stories are often limited in scope because of this pressure to move on to the next stories, journalists' increasing workloads due to shrinking newsrooms, and redefined job duties (Zamith and Braun 2019; Örnebring 2018). Collectively, this suggests that journalists cannot stick to a story for very long, even if technological barriers are removed, because of their limited capacity and the incentive to move on to the next big story.

In our context, the historic nature of the justices' decision to hold oral arguments remotely, as well as to livestream them, likely altered the news media's considerations regarding whether to cover these proceedings. Indeed, the change in the Court's format and media access was novel, involved a major government institution, and had the potential to impact the public at large. Livestreaming was a new technology for the Court that reduced the time for gathering information about oral arguments. Therefore, we anticipate that the immediate access to oral argument audio will correspond to an increase in coverage by news media.

As the novelty of the new format and availability of livestreamed oral argument audio wore off, however, we expect that this bump in the quantity of coverage will subside due to the quick pace of contemporary news cycles, the resource constraints faced by journalists, and competing opportunities for coverage. Further, while livestreamed audio is an unprecedented change for the Court, it does not substantively alter the news media's calculation regarding which cases to cover. Case attributes associated with newsworthiness, including the issue at stake and Solicitor General participation (e.g., Sill et al. 2013), are generally independent of whether oral arguments are livestreamed. While these proceedings provide insight into how the Court may rule (Black et al. 2011; Johnson 2004; Black, Johnson, and Wedeking 2012), these cues are present regardless of whether the audio is livestreamed. As a result, *we expect that livestreamed oral argument audio will initially increase news media coverage of oral arguments but that this change in coverage will dissipate in the long term.*

Beyond the frequency of news media coverage of oral arguments, we anticipate the availability of livestreamed audio will alter the *nature* of coverage by the news media in the short term but that this change will not continue in the long term. Specifically, we argue that there will be an increase in story word counts, direct quotes from the proceedings, and sentence-length quotes when the Court initially makes livestreamed audio available. The reason is that livestreamed audio provides instantaneous access to these proceedings in a manner that alters the tools available to Court reporters. This satisfies the quick pace of the twenty-four-hour news cycle (Vasterman 2005; Ritter 2020). Further, because oral argument is the first time the justices collectively consider the merits of a case (Black et al. 2012), the information exchanged during these proceedings offers valuable insights about how the justices will decide the legal and policy issues involved (Black et al. 2011; Johnson 2004; Black et al. 2012). In particular, the dialogue provides fodder for news media coverage, including the ideological direction of the decision, the justices' votes, and the potential use of judicial review (e.g., Sill et al. 2013; Zilis 2015). Immediate access to oral argument, and the ability to play back audio prior to a media deadline, may also change coverage because it reduces barriers to providing more detailed coverage.

However, the twenty-four-hour news cycle may constrain the media's ability to include more quotes or other nuances from the discussions in the long term. This is because, at some point, the novelty of livestreamed oral argument will wear off, and journalists will move on to the next big stories (Zamith and Braun 2019; Örnebring 2018). Thus, *we expect that livestreamed oral argument audio will alter the nature of coverage surrounding the initial May 2020 argument sessions but these alterations will not persist in the long term.*[42]

PLAN FOR THE BOOK

To test our two key hypotheses, we assembled a dataset of news media coverage of Supreme Court oral arguments from the October 2019 to May 2022 sessions.[43] Data that focuses on the coverage from these sessions allow us to assess whether the Court's transition to livestreaming changed the amount of media coverage and whether the nature of said coverage changed. We leave the detailed discussion of these data to chapter 1, which explicates the news media outlets on which we focus—the top US newspapers and television news organizations that report on political news—as well as how we coded each article as we created our dataset.

The remaining chapters lay out our argument. Chapter 2 focuses on the volume (or frequency) of coverage in online print media outlets. Here we lay out the massive increase in coverage of cases during the May 2020 argument session and the corresponding move back to normal when the justices continued this practice in October 2020. We conclude the chapter with a model that allows us to examine the specific factors that may increase the likelihood of case coverage. From there we turn to the nature and depth of coverage in chapter 3. The analysis here focuses on when and how the media quote directly from oral argument proceedings. It is this chapter that speaks directly to the justices' concern that putting cameras in the courtroom for argument sessions will lead to media coverage that may make the justices or the Court look bad. Finally, because the nature of broadcast media (i.e., stories run on news programs) differs from online print media, we parse out these outlets in chapter 4. Here, we conduct analyses similar to chapters 2 and 3—the amount and nature of coverage—from the nation's top broadcast outlets. Combined, these analyses build strong support for our hypotheses.

CONCLUSION

US Supreme Court justices enjoy their anonymity and know their institution is usually in the spotlight only when it issues opinions at the end of each term. But, like every other US institution, the justices had to adjust how they did work in response to the first pandemic in over a century. This book tells the story of how the nation's highest judicial institution adapted to the pandemic and describes the potential consequences of these adaptations. Our findings allow us to make claims about how other institutions will have to adjust when future crises strike the United States as COVID-19 did in 2020.

Chapter 1

Examining News Media Coverage of Supreme Court Oral Arguments

INTRODUCTION

The COVID-19 pandemic upended routines for every single person in the United States. Schools shut down; workplaces closed; and local, state, and federal officials issued restrictions on social contact including stay-at-home orders and curfews. Further, everyone was forced to navigate a new normal including lockdown and quarantine that led many people to work from home and home-school children in a new blended learning setting. Most dramatically, as Americans increasingly lived their entire lives from home, the internet became a classroom, a workplace, a meeting space, and even a dancefloor.[1]

Perhaps most importantly, the internet facilitated continued contact and collaboration through video and audio conferencing. These conference platforms became a venue for everything from celebrating holidays with family and friends to conducting remote meetings or visiting doctors. Zoom, for instance, had ten million daily meeting participants in December 2019 but by April 2020—just a month after President Donald Trump declared the coronavirus a national emergency—that number had risen to over 300 million (Evans 2020).[2] Other video conferencing platforms, including Google Meet and Microsoft Teams, experienced similar significant increases in daily participants (Peters 2020; Thorp-Lancaster 2020).[3] More broadly, Pew Research Center found that four out of every five Americans used a video or audio conferencing tool during the COVID-19 pandemic.[4] The point is that these digital conferencing tools helped people navigate life through the nation's first pandemic in more than a century.

And individuals were not alone in using digital conferencing technology. The government and, for our purposes, federal courts relied on video and audio conferencing to keep open civilian courts of law.[5] Since the pandemic initially closed many courts, the Judicial Conference of the United States temporarily approved the use of video and audio conferencing for certain criminal proceedings and allowed access through audio conferencing for civil proceedings.[6] Federal courts, like the public, needed a way to continue their day-to-day business, and by using video or audio conferencing they ensured cases were not backlogged. As the Honorable Judge Marsha J. Pechman put it, "I have no backlog. Every single case I had set in 2020 got tried in 2020." Pechman then summed up the situation in this way: "I tell my fellow judges this may be the only way the wheels of justice will still turn."[7]

The US Supreme Court was in a predicament similar to US District and US Circuit courts. During its October 2019 Term, the justices placed seventy-three cases on their docket for arguments. As we note in the Introduction, the Court typically hears oral arguments in such cases from the first Monday in October until the end of April of the following year. However, due to the pandemic—and the ensuing lockdowns—its oral argument schedule came to an abrupt halt in March of 2020. Specifically, it postponed all arguments scheduled for the March session (March 23–25 and March 30–April 1) and closed its doors to the public until further notice. In a press release, the justices made clear this postponement was not unprecedented. Indeed, they pointed to the fact that, prior to the 2020 pandemic, the Court had postponed arguments scheduled for October 1918 in response to the Spanish flu epidemic and also shortened its argument calendars in August 1793 and August 1798 in response to yellow fever outbreaks.[8]

While postponing arguments was not unprecedented, the Court's next move *was*. In a follow-up press release, on April 13, 2020, the Court joined lower federal courts in an historic move. Because it was now backlogged with cases the justices believed they needed to hear and decide, they chose to change the process so they could hear arguments remotely via telephonic audio conference. Important for our analysis, as the press release in figure 1.1 shows, while the arguments would be held over the phone, the Court also anticipated "providing a live audio feed of these arguments to news media." In what follows, we briefly describe how its move to embrace this technology during the pandemic changed how citizens and the media were exposed to the Court's arguments. We then turn to an explanation of the data we use to systematically test our hypotheses of interest concerning how the amount and content of media coverage changed because of the decision to provide a live feed of the argument sessions.

For Immediate Release
April 13, 2020

For Further Information Contact:
Kathleen Arberg (202) 479-3211

The Court will hear oral arguments by telephone conference on May 4, 5, 6, 11, 12 and 13 in a limited number of previously postponed cases. The following cases will be assigned argument dates after the Clerk's Office has confirmed the availability of counsel:

18-9526, *McGirt v. Oklahoma*

19-46, *United States Patent and Trademark Office v. Booking.com B.V.*

19-177, *Agency for International Development v. Alliance for Open Society International, Inc.*

19-267, *Our Lady of Guadalupe School v. Morrissey-Berru*, and 19-348, *St. James School v. Biel*

19-431, *Little Sisters of the Poor Saints Peter and Paul Home v. Pennsylvania*, and 19-454, *Trump v. Pennsylvania*

19-465, *Chiafalo v. Washington*

19-518, *Colorado Department of State v. Baca*

19-631, *Barr v. American Association of Political Consultants, Inc.*

19-635, *Trump v. Vance*

19-715, *Trump v. Mazars USA, LLP*, and 19-760, *Trump v. Deutsche Bank AG*

In keeping with public health guidance in response to COVID-19, the Justices and counsel will all participate remotely. The Court anticipates providing a live audio feed of these arguments to news media. Details will be shared as they become available.

The Court Building remains open for official business, but most Court personnel are teleworking. The Court Building remains closed to the public until further notice.

Figure 1.1   Press Release from US Supreme Court Public Information Office Announcing Livestreamed Arguments. *Source*: https://www.supremecourt.gov/publicinfo/press/press-releases/pr_04-13-20

THE MEDIA AND THE PUBLIC'S EXPOSURE TO LIVESTREAMED ARGUMENTS

As we discussed in the Introductory Chapter, during a typical oral argument day at the Court, seating is extremely limited for both the press and the public. For the press, only thirty-six seats in the Court's oral argument chambers are reserved for members of the press (Howe 2020). This means only a select few reporters are permitted to attend, in person, the Court's proceedings. Further, electronic devices of any kind, such as cameras, cell phones, and laptops, are not allowed in the courtroom (Schubert et al. 1992; Wasby et al. 1976; Carter 2012). Thus, even for those who can attend an argument, they must take copious notes that they then use to write up stories after arguments end.

Space is also limited in the courtroom for the general public. For typical arguments, this means fewer than fifty seats are available in the courtroom for citizens (Peters 2013). For most of the public, then, the only way to learn about what transpired during an argument is to wait for the Court to release the audio or written transcripts, or to wait for information provided by print, broadcast, or streaming media outlets.

Ultimately, neither the media nor the public has historically had *unlimited* access to the Court's arguments—seats are restricted and the Court has historically held onto its transcripts and audio of the proceedings until hours or days have passed. However, with the availability of livestreamed oral argument audio, access to the Court transformed overnight. Rather than waiting to hear delayed, and often second-hand, accounts of what transpired during arguments, livestreaming opened the Court's doors, in real time, to anyone interested in listening. Thus, with livestreaming, people could simply use their laptops, cell phones, or any other digital device to listen as the justices and attorneys battled out cases.[9]

Consider figure 1.2 which offers a glimpse into what the first livestreamed oral argument looked like for people and media outlets who observed via C-SPAN's website. In *US Patent & Trademark Office v. Booking.com* (2020), listeners were able to follow a real-time transcript of argument—similar to closed captioning provided on television and streaming services—and C-SPAN displayed an image of whomever was talking at a particular time to help the public and media follow the discussion. Here, Justice Stephen Breyer was engaging in questioning with Lisa Blatt, the attorney arguing for Booking.com. And, instead of holding discussion as only several hundred audience members listened in the courtroom, Breyer and Blatt were talking to one another in a digital courtroom with potentially millions of people in the virtual gallery.[10]

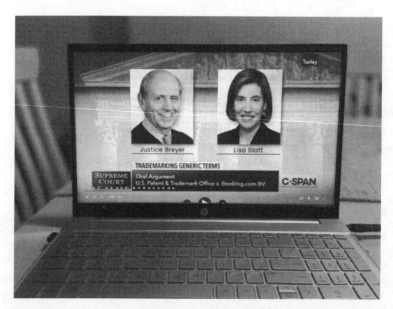

Figure 1.2   What C-SPAN Livestreaming Viewers Saw on May 4, 2020 When Justice Stephen Breyer and Attorney Lisa Blatt Interacted during Oral Arguments in *U.S. Patent & Trademark Office v. Booking.com* (2020). Credit: Rachael Houston, Fort Worth Texas.

This access to the Court's arguments fundamentally changed how the media engaged with it. We are particularly interested in how access changed the ability to report on arguments about cases the justices decide because, rather than the media having to wait until the end of the day for an official transcript of argument, or until the end of the week to access the argument audio, media outlets had real-time access to all the Court's proceedings. This, in turn, allowed them the opportunity to begin crafting, writing, and editing stories using close to real-time quotes from the justices and attorneys. In so doing, they could refer to specific interactions among the justices and between the justices and the attorneys, and provide immediate in-depth details about the cases as the argument continued. Our goal, then, is to determine how this direct and immediate access may have influenced how much, and in what ways, the media covered the Court's arguments. To do so, we compare media coverage of oral arguments before the Court offered such access with coverage from the May 2020 session (when livestreaming began) and beyond. In what follows, we describe how we gathered the data to make this comparison and how we coded for such changes in coverage.

Collecting Data on News Outlets That Cover the Court

Because we are interested in media coverage before and after the Court adopted livestreaming, we assembled a large dataset containing news media coverage of oral arguments from October 2019 through May 2022. In other words, we collected data spanning three full Court terms (i.e., the October 2019, 2020, and 2021 Terms). Our dataset therefore contains 20 argument sessions across these terms, totaling 174 individual cases.[11] Five of the sessions, from October 2019 to February 2020, took place *before* livestreaming began and the remaining fifteen sessions (including the May 2020 session) occurred *after* the Court began livestreaming. In total, this allows us to compare five sessions of traditional arguments without livestreaming to fifteen sessions of livestreamed arguments. This, in turn, permits us to determine whether, and how, livestreaming may (or may not) have impacted coverage of the Court's arguments in the short term and in the long term.

The media outlets on which we focus are the top ten US newspapers by average weekday paid circulation (including digital circulation for 2019) and the top eight US television news organizations that report on political news by viewership.[12] We took this tack because we wanted to cast our net over a broad range of media attention to the Court's oral arguments—guaranteeing we captured "mainstream" coverage of the Court and its arguments.[13] We chose to examine two types of coverage—online print and broadcast—because research demonstrates people have different motivations for engaging these two mediums when they obtain news (Shah, McLeod, and Yoon 2001) and each attracts different groups of viewers or readers (Chaffee and Frank 1996). Moreover, the information provided in the two mediums varies significantly as television news segments, on average, contain fewer words and offer less in-depth coverage than print news stories. The reason is that broadcast messages must be immediately understood so their stories need to be shorter than print or online versions of print stories. As Yopp and McAdams (2007) write, "Writing for television news must also capture attention quickly because TV messages can breeze by passive audiences who do not rewind or re-read items of interest" (256). For these reasons, we divide our main dataset into two separate ones: an online print news coverage dataset (that we utilize in chapters 2 and 3) and a broadcast news coverage dataset (that we utilize in chapter 4).

Table 1.1 displays all of the news outlets in our dataset. By including eighteen outlets across twenty Supreme Court oral argument sessions, this is arguably the most comprehensive analysis to date of how the media report on these proceedings. This, in turn provides us with insights about media coverage of the Court's transition to livestreaming and about coverage of oral arguments more generally. It also compares sharply with the vast majority of prior literature that simply examines how the media covers Court decisions (e.g., Hoekstra 2003; Slotnick and Segal 1998; but see, e.g., Clark et al. 2014). Further, existing analyses of the Court and media tend to exclusively examine newspaper coverage (e.g., Ericson 1977; Haider-Markel et al. 2006).

Our approach also provides us with a broad range of media outlets in terms of ideological diversity. This ensures that we can speak about Court media coverage generally and not exclusively from one side of the political or ideological aisle. Indeed, we include newspapers and broadcast networks that lean conservative (e.g., *New York Post*, Fox News), lean liberal (e.g., CNN, *The Washington Post*), and are in the center (e.g., *USA Today*,

Table 1.1   Media Outlets Included in Oral Argument Media Coverage Dataset

Top Ten Newspapers	Top Eight Broadcast Networks
USA Today	NBC News
The Wall Street Journal	CBS News
The New York Times	ABC News
New York Post	Fox News
Los Angeles Times	PBS
The Washington Post	MSNBC
Star Tribune	CNN
Newsday	Fox Business Network
Chicago Tribune	
The Boston Globe	

Table 1.2 Ideological Leanings of News Outlets Included in Oral Argument Media Coverage Dataset (data based on the Interactive Media Bias Charts: https://adfontesmedia.com/interactive-media-bias-chart/)

Media Outlet	Ideological Leaning
USA Today	Center
The Wall Street Journal	Center
Star Tribune	Center
Newsday	Center
Chicago Tribune	Center
CBS News	Center
ABC News	Center
PBS	Center
New York Post	Conservative Leaning
Fox News	Conservative Leaning
Fox Business Network	Conservative Leaning
The New York Times	Liberal Leaning
Los Angeles Times	Liberal Leaning
The Washington Post	Liberal Leaning
The Boston Globe	Liberal Leaning
NBC News	Liberal Leaning
MSNBC	Liberal Leaning
CNN	Liberal Leaning

ABC News). To make this clear, table 1.2 displays the same news outlets as depicted in table 1.1 except, this time, with the outlets arranged by their ideological leanings according to the Media Bias Chart—a tool that rates news for reliability and bias.[14]

Beyond ideological diversity, using top media outlets by circulation and viewership also provides variation in terms of regional diversity. Specifically, we include media outlets from across the United States including Minneapolis (*Star Tribune*), Boston (*The Boston Globe*), Los Angeles (*Los Angeles Times*), New York (*Fox News* and Fox Business Network), and Atlanta (CNN). Collectively, news source, ideology, and region all contribute to our diverse set of news outlets (Joris et al. 2020). Next, we discuss the datasets we constructed: online print news and broadcast news.

Online Print News Coverage Data Collection

In our online print news coverage dataset, we gathered all *online* stories from every one of the eighteen media outlets depicted in table 1.1. We focus on newspaper outlets' *online presence* instead of their physical print presence because newspaper subscriber bases have been in decline since the mid-2000s while their website audience traffic has grown.[15] Moreover, a large majority of US adults (82 percent) say they often or sometimes obtain news from a smartphone, computer, or tablet, whereas fewer than 5 percent of individuals obtain the same news from a traditional newspaper.[16] We also collected online print news stories (which we distinguish from their broadcast news transcripts) from our television networks of interest because data from the Pew Research Center indicates that people prefer to access news from digital platforms instead of from television. In fact, digital platforms are the most popular place for people to obtain their news.[17] With this dataset, we capture the influence newspapers and television outlets have in the digital space, at least when it comes to coverage of oral arguments at the US Supreme Court.

To gather our online news stories of interest, we navigated to the website of each news outlet listed in table 1.1. We then typed the keywords "Supreme Court argument [INSERT CASE NAME]" into the search bar and repeated this step for every orally argued case during our terms of interest. Further, because the press often uses shorthand for case names, or refers to the parties as either petitioner or respondent in their coverage, we also searched "Supreme Court argument [INSERT PETITIONER NAME IN CASE]" and "Supreme Court argument [INSERT RESPONDENT'S NAME IN CASE]." In total, for each of the 18 media outlets in our dataset, we performed 522 searches—three searches for every case in our dataset. Collectively, this amounts to 9,396 online searches across the online print media outlets. Finally, note that we also searched the term "Supreme Court argument" more broadly on each news outlet's website for each day of oral argument across our twenty sessions of interest. Doing so accounted for approximately 3,000 more searches.

Not every search was this easy, however. If a case name had a generic petitioner or defendant, such as United States in *Kelly v. United States* (2020) or *United States v. Sineneng-Smith* (2020), we double checked the date and content of each article to ensure its focus was on the relevant oral argument. For consolidated cases, we used the same search criteria and added any articles to the case caption listed on the Court's docket. For example, on February 24, 2020, the Court heard arguments for *U.S. Forest Service v. Cowpasture River Assn.* (2020) and *Atlantic Coast Pipeline, LLC v. Cowpasture River Assn. (Consolidated)* (2020). We included all articles returned with our search criteria for *Atlantic Coast Pipeline, LLC* under *U.S. Forest Service*.

For the October 2019 to March 2020 sessions (before livestreaming commenced), we searched with the above criteria on the date each oral argument session occurred and on the Friday of each argument week because this is when the Court released audio of the entire week's arguments (see the Introductory Chapter). However, for the May 2020 session and beyond, we only collected stories on the date the case was argued, as the audio was live and available immediately to news outlets.[18] We then compiled these news stories, including their titles, URLs, and story content, into a spreadsheet. Combined, this means our online print news database includes print articles produced by traditional print outlets, like *The Washington Post*, and broadcast outlets like CNN that also have print/digital coverage. It also includes original coverage from each outlet, and coverage reprinted from the Associated Press or other major news outlets. In total, we collected 644 online print news stories across the twenty argument sessions we analyze.

Table 1.3 breaks down the online print coverage by media outlet. Three newspapers dominate—*The New York Times*, *The Washington Post*, and *The Wall Street Journal* account for about 30 percent of all the coverage. CNN comes in fourth, producing 7.6 percent of the stories. This is an interesting finding given that CNN also produces the most broadcast news stories about the Court's oral arguments (which we discuss in the next section). MSNBC, Fox Business, and Newsday provide the least amount of coverage.

Once we identified all the stories about the oral argument for each case of interest, research assistants worked independently to code specific details about each story. Specifically, we gave them a codebook that specified the coding and categorizing protocol (Riffe et al. 2005).[19] Using this tool, they coded for the word count of each story (*BodyWordCount*), whether the story was written by someone at the news outlet (*OriginalStory*), if it was an opinion piece (*OpinionStory*), and whether the story contained any quotes from the justices or the attorneys during argument (*Quote*).[20] Research assistants also specified to whom each quote was attributed (Chief Justice John Roberts

Table 1.3   Percentage of Stories in the Dataset Produced about Orally Argued Cases by Each Online Print News Outlet (2019–2021 Terms)

Online Print Media Outlet	Percentage (%)
The New York Times	12.58
The Washington Post	10.40
The Wall Street Journal	8.39
CNN	7.61
USA Today	7.30
ABC	7.14
Fox	6.99
Los Angeles Times	6.83
NBC	6.83
CBS	4.97
PBS	4.81
New York Post	3.88
Star Tribune	3.57
The Boston Globe	2.80
Chicago Tribune	2.33
MSNBC	1.40
Fox Business	1.24
Newsday	0.93
Total (N = 644)	100.00

or Associate Justices Samuel Alito, Sonia Sotomayor, Clarence Thomas, Ruth Bader Ginsburg, Brett Kavanaugh, Neil Gorsuch, Stephen Breyer, Elena Kagan, or Amy Coney Barrett). They then coded quote-specific variables, including whether the quote was at least one full sentence (*Full*) or whether it was less than a complete sentence (*Partial*), whether the quote is part of an exchange between a justice and an advocate (*AdvocateExchange*) or between two or more justices (*JusticeExchange*), and whether the justices are quoted when they ask a specific question (*Question*).[21]

Because these variables are not qualitatively subjective (e.g., the degree to which the stories are persuasive, the extent to which they frame the justices in a positive or negative way), we did not need to conduct formal intercoder reliability tests. That is, there was no debate between the research assistants as to how to interpret and code these variables. However, to be sure mistakes were not made, we had three separate research assistants code the same variables for each story and then we cross-checked each coding to make sure they were the same. If there was a discrepancy across assistants, we addressed it and used a consensus decision-making criteria to choose the proper coding. We discuss each of these variables at greater lengths in chapters 2, 3, and 4.

Consider, for example, an online print news story from CNN covering the Court's arguments in *Dobbs v. Jackson Women's Health Organization* (2022).[22] This story contains 1,347 words, is original because it is written by a CNN reporter (Ariane de Vogue), is not an opinion piece, and contains quotes from Roberts, Kavanaugh, Alito, Sotomayor, Breyer, Mississippi Solicitor General Scott Stewart, US Solicitor General Elizabeth Prelogar, and lawyers for Jackson Women's Health Organization. The article quotes Roberts as saying that fifteen weeks is not a "dramatic departure" from the definition of viability for a fetus. Further, we code the quote as partial because it contains only two words and is not at least one full sentence and was an exchange between a justice and an advocate (Julie Rikelman for the respondent—Jackson Women's Health Organization). We also coded this as a statement made by Roberts rather than as a question he asked. In this manner, our research assistants coded every quote contained in all 644 stories in our online print news dataset.

Broadcast News Coverage Data Collection

Our dataset of broadcast news coverage contains only broadcast stories from the eight television networks listed in table 1.1. The reason we made this choice is that the newspapers in our dataset do not have a presence on broadcast television, whereas the broadcast networks in our dataset do have an online print presence. For example, CNN produces television broadcasts and also writes online print stories. In contrast, *The New York Times* only writes online print stories. The other reason we collected broadcast data separately is that, behind digital news (53 percent), television is people's second most preferred platform to receive news (33 percent).[23] Consequently, with this choice we capture media attention to the Court using the two most popular news formats for public consumption of news: online print news and television news.

We followed Hitt and Searles' (2018) data collection method that relies on LexisNexis Academic (LNA). This database includes over 17,000 news, business, and legal sources. We searched for the keywords "Supreme Court" and "argument" on the website, selecting the filter for broadcast news, and divided our search into the argument session from October 2019 to May 2022. For example, the May 2020 session includes cases heard by the Court between May 4 and May 13, 2020. In short, for this session we searched LexisNexis using the keywords "Supreme Court" and "argument" between these two dates.[24]

We gathered and stored the transcripts from all the television media organizations listed in table 1.2.[25] As with the online print outlets, a team of research assistants sorted through the compiled stories using the search criteria "Supreme Court" and "argument," pulled only the stories that discussed these proceedings, and then compiled them in a spreadsheet. We had to sort through the stories collected from LNA because sometimes news outlets previewed an oral argument that would occur months later or discuss one that occurred in years previous. Like our online print dataset, we collected broadcast stories that occurred on the day of an argument and on the Friday of each argument week for cases argued prior to livestreaming because this is when the Court typically released audio of the week's arguments. However, for the May 2020 session and beyond we only collected stories on the date a case was argued.

Below we provide an example of a transcript as it appears after searching the LNA database:

Johnson & Johnson Asks FDA To Authorize Booster Shots; Sen. Mike Braun (R-IN) Is Interviewed About Debt Limit; Soon: Biden Arrives In Michigan To Pitch Economic Agenda. Aired 12:30-1p ET

CNN Transcripts | Oct 05, 2021 | NEWS; Domestic | 3107 | John King, Leana Wen, Melanie Zanona, Seung Min Kim
… again, Clarence Thomas, unusually chatty.
KING: Topping our Political Radar today for the second day in a row Justice Clarence Thomas asked the first question during oral arguments at the Supreme Court today. The new involvement of the usually quiet…
… it is important, but first you got to figure out how much are we going to spend and then you figure out how to divvy it up as we go. Appreciate

everybody coming in. [12:54:09] So when we come back, the second day of the
new Supreme Court term and yet...
    ... argue that you should retire as soon as possible while the Democrats have
the Senate Majority? That's the basic issue that those protesters –
    JUSTICE STEPHEN BREYER, SUPREME COURT: Well, that's their point
of view. I've said pretty much what I have to...
    justice comes at a very significant time. On the docket this fall several
monumental cases including abortion and gun rights. Justice Stephen Breyer
says the return to in-person arguments at the court is in his view, a big
improvement over doing business . . .[26]

Within the LNA database, search results include a link to the full broadcast
story, the title of the story, and the shows where the terms "argument" and
"Supreme Court" are used. In this story, dated October 5, 2021, CNN reported
that Thomas asked the first question during oral arguments at the Supreme
Court. In fact, on this day he asked the first question in both argued cases. This
is newsworthy because, as we discuss at greater length later in the book, for
years Thomas rarely posed questions in the courtroom (see, e.g., Johnson et al.
2021). However, unlike online print news stories, this broadcast story does
not dedicate much time to discussing the substance of the Court's arguments.
    Once we clicked on the hyperlink at the top of the transcript to view the
full story, this point became clear. Indeed, the (very short) excerpt from the
news broadcast that discusses the Court's arguments in these cases is shown
below:[27]

So when we come back, the second day of the new Supreme Court term and yet
again, Clarence Thomas, unusually chatty.
    (COMMERCIAL BREAK)
    KING: Topping our Political Radar today for the second day in a row Justice
Clarence Thomas asked the first question during oral arguments at the Supreme
Court today. The new involvement of the usually quiet justice comes at a very
significant time. On the docket this fall several monumental cases including
abortion and gun rights.
    Justice Stephen Breyer says the return to in-person arguments at the court
is in his view, a big improvement over doing business virtually throwing a
wide-ranging interview with CNN's Joan Biskupic. The senior liberal was also
heckled by protesters who want the 83-year-old to retire. His response
    (BEGIN VIDEO CLIP)
    JOAN BISKUPIC, CNN LEGAL ANALYST: What do you say to people
who argue that you should retire as soon as possible while the Democrats have
the Senate Majority? That's the basic issue that those protesters—
    JUSTICE STEPHEN BREYER, SUPREME COURT: Well, that's their
point of view. I've said pretty much what I have to say.
    (END VIDEO CLIP)[28]

While this news story certainly discusses the proceedings, it does so with very little detail. This is the case across almost all the broadcast news stories in our dataset. In fact, here, only two sentences, and a total of forty-one words, are dedicated to discussing the oral arguments. This contrasts with the online print story—discussed in the previous section—that contains 1,347 words. The point is that when broadcast outlets produce news stories about the oral argument, they offer far less detail than online print stories. As a result, we coded these stories slightly differently than we did online print sources.

In particular, for each of the 282 broadcast stories that met our criteria (i.e., it was about oral argument and ran on the relevant dates), we copied the news story, title, and content into a spreadsheet. Again, a team of research assistants used a codebook that specified the coding and categorizing protocol (Riffe et al. 2005). For instance, they coded the news outlet that produced the broadcast story (*News_Outlet*) and organized the stories by argument session. However, we did not code the stories in the same explicit manner as we did the online print stories because the information provided is so limited across broadcast stories. Specifically, none of the broadcast stories directly quoted the justices or advocates, and we could not collect data on whether the stories were original or if they were opinion pieces. We were, however, able to perform textual analysis on them, which we discuss, and use, in chapter 4. In all, our online print dataset is much more comprehensive than the broadcast data due to the more in-depth nature of these stories.

Table 1.4 depicts the breakdown of broadcast stories about oral arguments produced by each outlet in our dataset. CNN provides the most airtime for the Court's proceedings across all our sessions of interest. In fact, it accounts for almost half of the coverage while its conservative counterpart, Fox News, does not cover the Court's oral arguments to the same extent. In fact, it produces only about 9 percent of the broadcast stories. More ideological centrist news outlets, including CBS, ABC, and PBS, account for almost a quarter of the coverage of interest.

Table 1.4   Percentage of Stories in the Dataset Produced about Orally Argued Cases by Each Broadcast News Outlet (2019–2021 Terms)

Broadcast Media Outlet	Percentage (%)
CNN	46.80
MSNBC	16.31
PBS	10.28
CBS News	9.93
Fox News	8.87
ABC	4.26
NBC	3.55
Total (N = 282)	100.00

General Oral Argument and Case-Level Data Collection

Our main focus throughout the remainder of the book is on how the change to livestreamed arguments may have altered the volume and nature of media coverage of Supreme Court oral arguments. However, we must account for other factors that may also affect this relationship. Specifically, existing data demonstrate that the salience of cases the Court hears affects media coverage of them (see, e.g., Slotnick and Segal 1998; Maltzman et al. 2000; Johnson 2004). Thus, we collected additional data for a variety of salience measures for each of the 174 cases across our 20 sessions of interest that may affect the coverage of a case.

First, we create a measure of case salience based on Clark et al. (2014). Because our interest is with the date of oral argument, we only count media coverage *prior to* the actual proceedings (rather than prior to the date a decision is handed down). This variable, *Pre-Argument Stories,* takes on an integer value for the number of stories from all three news outlets (*The New York Times, The Washington Post,* and *The Los Angeles Times*) about each case.[29] In our statistical models in chapters 2 and 3, we include this measure of salience to account for the fact that media outlets may have been particularly interested in several key cases that were postponed but ultimately argued in May 2020, including *Little Sisters of the Poor Saints Peter and Paul Home v. Pennsylvania* (2020)—the ongoing conflict over the Affordable Care Act and the Religious Freedom Restoration Act—and *Trump v. Vance* (2020)—the case surrounding whether a US District Court could subpoena then-President Donald Trump.

Second, we counted the number of times each justice spoke during a specific argument session because it is seen as a key measure of justices' personal views of case salience (see Black et al. 2012). We captured this variable, *Number of Turns,* by downloading every argument transcript and then summing individual justice utterances to obtain a total for each case. Next, the issue involved in a case is often used as a proxy for a case's legal salience. Existing work demonstrates that civil liberties and constitutional cases are considered more salient than other cases (Maltzman et al. 2000). Thus, we code for whether an argument involved a *Civil Liberties Case* or a *Constitutional Case* (coded 1) according to the Supreme Court Data Base (Spaeth et al. 2022). Finally, we code *Solicitor General* 1 if the Solicitor General's office was involved directly in a case as a named party or if they supported the petitioners or respondents during argument as *amicus curiae.* Evidence demonstrates that Solicitor General involvement signals a case is salient for the federal government (Black and Owens 2012).

CONCLUSION

In this chapter, we laid out how we will examine the relationship between the media and the Court when the former was allowed to listen to oral arguments in real time. Because of the immediate access to the Court's arguments, we explored the data to determine how the volume and nature of media coverage may have changed as a result. With these data in hand, we now provide a rich understanding of exactly how media coverage changed (or did not change) across online print news stories and broadcast stories.

Chapter 2

Did Livestreamed Arguments Increase Online Print Media Coverage of Supreme Court Oral Arguments?

INTRODUCTION

The US government recognizes eleven federal holidays.[1] Of course, other days may also be important enough to garner this distinction and, within the last decade, several have been proposed.[2] To our knowledge, however, no public official has suggested designating the first Monday in October as a federal holiday.[3] But perhaps it should enjoy such a designation because, each year, this day commemorates the beginning of the US Supreme Court's new term wherein the justices commence the process of hearing oral arguments. Further, this day often garners a great deal of media attention and, according to C-SPAN's archives, it enjoys a prodigious number of listeners for the first cases argued during a new term (whether before or after livestreaming began in 2020).[4]

While excitement is always palpable among Court watchers in the days leading up to the First Monday of October, such excitement pales in comparison to the broad interest in May of 2020 when the justices restarted its 2019 Term by hearing arguments despite the ongoing pandemic. Indeed, when we conducted a simple Google News search of news articles published from April 15, 2020, to May 15, 2020 (using the search phrase "Supreme Court to livestream arguments"), we found more than 2,000 of them devoted to the justices' decision to allow people outside the courtroom to listen live to its arguments for the first time in the Court's history. Further, as Houston and Johnson (2023) demonstrate, more than 42,000 people navigated to the C-SPAN website to listen to the inaugural livestreamed proceedings in *Patent & Trademark v. Booking.com* (2020).[5] Further, *Booking.com* garnered almost triple the listeners compared to many higher salience cases argued during May 2020.[6]

Our point is that the public seemed overwhelmingly excited, and ready, for the Court to allow immediate access to its arguments. For our phenomenon of interest, coverage of these proceedings, the media were just as excited based on their significant and wide-ranging coverage of these cases. But *how does this coverage compare to pre-pandemic argument coverage when the Court held arguments with no livestreaming and to coverage of cases held as it continued livestreaming when arguments resumed in October 2020?* To answer this question, we compare online print media coverage of cases argued during May 2020 with coverage of pre-pandemic orally argued cases during the October 2019 Term (with no livestreaming) and with cases argued from the proceeding October 2020 and October 2021 Terms (when livestreaming continued).[7]

The chapter proceeds as follows. First, we provide a brief recap of our argument and our volume (frequency) hypotheses. From there we analyze the descriptive data as a preliminary test of them. We then turn to a more systematic analysis of the factors that lead the media to cover Supreme Court oral arguments during our time period of interest. Finally, we offer some concluding remarks about what these data say about when and why the media increase coverage of this part of the justices' decision-making process.

OVERVIEW OF COVERAGE FREQUENCY ARGUMENT

As we note in the introduction, the availability of livestreamed oral argument audio clearly increased *access* to these proceedings. But does such access also change the *volume* of online print media coverage? Livingston and Bennett (2003) suggest it could. Indeed, they focus on technology that may help reduce the time it takes to deliver content and argue that the immediacy of information flow can shape what news outlets decide to cover. For our purpose, livestreaming is a technology that reduced the time it took the media to gather information about the Supreme Court's oral arguments.[8] Practically, this meant media outlets could immediately report on information about evolving case arguments, which may have been a consideration for them when deciding how much focus to place on these proceedings. The reason for such consideration is that now, more than ever, people want to be informed as soon as possible about relevant changes in their world (Drok and Hermans 2016). In turn, journalists consider fast dissemination of news to be one of their most important tasks when determining what stories to cover (Weaver and Willnat 2012).

In our context, the historic nature of the justices' decision to livestream oral arguments likely altered the news media's decisions about whether, and how much, to cover these proceedings. On a general level, the change in media access was novel, involved a major government institution, and had the potential to impact the public at large. Further, livestreaming was a new technology that reduced the time for gathering information about oral arguments. Therefore, we anticipate that *the immediate access to oral argument audio will correspond to an increase in coverage by online print news media.*

However, as the novelty of the new format and availability of livestreamed oral argument audio wore off, we expect this increase in coverage to subside due to the quick pace of contemporary news cycles, the resource constraints faced by journalists, and competing opportunities for coverage. In other words, *we expect that livestreamed oral argument audio will initially increase online print news media coverage of oral arguments but that this change in coverage will dissipate in the long term.*

DESCRIPTIVE DATA

To test these hypotheses, we utilize the data outlined in chapter 1. We do so through a variety of lenses. First, we assess our general phenomenon of interest—the overall volume (frequency) with which online print media covered cases during the oral argument sessions in our sample. These initial findings lead us to examine the data a bit more explicitly. Thus, we next consider which individual case arguments garnered the most online print media coverage. Finally, we examine whether online print outlets in our sample, from points across the ideological spectrum, varied in how they responded to the Court's move to livestreamed arguments.

The Volume of Online Print Media Coverage

We turn first to a 30,000-foot view of the data in figure 2.1. This figure focuses on the *volume* of oral argument coverage before May 2020 (gray bars to the left of the black bar), during May 2020 (the black bar), and after May 2020 (the gray bars to the right of the black bar). One need only eyeball the figure to determine a clear pattern. Initially, at the highest level of generality, it suggests a stark difference between the May 2020 argument session (when the Court began livestreaming arguments) and its sessions prior to livestreaming (October, November, December of 2019 and January and February of 2020), held during the same term.[9] This comports with our first hypothesis. In addition, and consistent with our second hypothesis, there is also a marked distinction between the May 2020 livestreamed arguments and the livestreamed sessions held during the October 2020 and 2021 Terms.

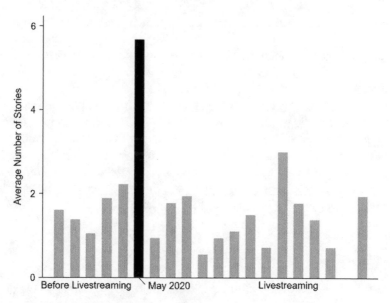

Figure 2.1   Average Number of Online Print Media Stories about Orally Argued Cases (2019–2021 Terms).

A closer examination of the data in figure 2.1 demonstrates that, among the eighteen online print media outlets in our dataset, each ran an average of 1.6 stories per case argued during the 2019 Term in-person sessions. In contrast, they ran an average of 5.7 stories for each of the ten cases argued in May 2020—despite the session taking place in the midst of the early months of the COVID-19 pandemic. Statistically, a difference of means test between these grouping of cases indicates there is clearly more online print media coverage of those ten cases ($p < 0.01$) than of the forty-eight cases argued prior in the term. This finding offers initial support for our first hypothesis *that media coverage increased when reporters could first listen to arguments in real time.*

In terms of our second hypothesis, we assess how the May 2020 session compares to livestreamed cases argued when the justices convened for the 2020 Term (beginning October 5, 2020) and for the 2021 Term (beginning October 4, 2021). The results are also as we expected. That is, online print media outlets ran an average of only 1.3 articles about cases argued during the post-May 2020 livestreamed sessions compared to the 5.7 that ran during that extraordinary May session. This difference is also statistically significant ($p < 0.01$), which provides preliminary support for our hypothesis *that the volume (or frequency) of news media coverage reverted to pre-pandemic levels after May 2020* as the media (and presumably the public) simply acclimated to the instant access provided by livestreaming arguments.

Beyond a first impression of the data, we note that every case argued during the first livestreamed session received coverage while this is not true for arguments held before or after May 2020. This is a noteworthy finding because not all cases argued during that month were highly salient (see our discussion of how we measure salience using *Pre-Argument Stories* in chapter 1). By this we mean that even cases that were not controversial, or that did not garner much attention prior to the argument day, still enjoyed widespread media coverage if they were argued during the first month of livestreaming. In particular, cases with few articles written about them prior to the day of oral argument—*Little Sisters of the Poor v. Pennsylvania* (2020), *McGirt v. Oklahoma* (2020), and *Barr, Atty Gen v. American Assn. of Political Consultants, Inc.* (2020)—had twenty-two, thirteen, and fourteen articles written about them on the day they were argued, respectively, despite the fact that they also only garnered two, one, and zero articles written about them prior to the argument day.

These findings hold even when we compare cases in our sample that have similar levels of salience. For example, compare a relatively low salience case argued during May 2020—*Chiafalo v. Washington* (2020)—with a case of similar salience argued prior to the beginning of livestreaming—*Department of Homeland Security v. Thuraissigiam* (2020). The former enjoyed twenty-four articles written about it while the latter enjoyed four times less coverage (six total articles). However, both had four articles (a relatively low number in our sample) written about them prior to their argument days. Similarly, when we compare cases that had a comparable number of pre-argument articles written about them from the initial month of livestreaming with cases argued after the initial month of livestreaming, the media again provided more oral argument coverage for the case heard during May 2020. Indeed, *Trump v. Mazars* (2020) and *Dobbs v. Jackson Women's Health Org.* (2022) are both considered highly salient, yet *Mazars* had seven more articles written about its oral argument than did *Dobbs* (twenty-six to nineteen).

Our point, with these data and examples, is that the media clearly paid extra attention to the May 2020 cases precisely because they were argued during such an unprecedented session when they could, for the first time in the Court's history, report on arguments in real time. And, while the level of case salience clearly has something to do with whether media covered oral arguments, the newsworthiness of the first month of livestreaming played a key role in the decision to publish articles during this period.[10]

Which Specific Cases Garnered the Most Coverage?

The findings in the previous section lead us to contemplate which specific cases in our sample enjoyed the most coverage when the advocates engaged with the justices during oral arguments. Table 2.1 allows us to answer this question as it depicts the most covered cases (with May 2020 cases in bold italics), which we operationalize as the number of stories produced by online print media outlets on the day a case was argued. At first glance it is evident that, while they do not comprise a majority of the list, every single case from May 2020 makes it into the top twenty-five. More telling is that half of the top ten cases (including ties) emanate from this session and all of them reach the top fifteen (with ties) in terms of coverage. Overall, the May 2020 cases comprise just under one-third of the top twenty-five most covered cases in our sample. This is fairly good evidence that online print media outlets were more likely to provide coverage of cases once they could produce real-time content. But perhaps these cases enjoyed more coverage because they were simply high-salience cases, as we insinuate at the end of the previous section. Fortunately, this table also allows us to determine the veracity of this claim.

Table 2.1 Top Twenty-Five Most Covered Orally Argued Cases by Online Print Media Outlets (2019–2021 Terms)

Case Name	OA Session	Number of Stories	Pre-Argument Stories
Patent & Trademark v. Booking.com	*May 2020*	*27*	*3*
Trump v. Mazars/ Trump v. Vance	*May 2020*	*26*	*23*
Chiafalo v. Washington	*May 2020*	*24*	*4*
Little Sisters of the Poor v. Pennsylvania	*May 2020*	*22*	*2*
Dobbs v. Jackson Women's Health Org.	Dec. 2021	19	28
Kennedy v. Bremerton School Dist.	Apr. 2022	19	5
Seila Law LLC v. CPB	Feb. 2020	15	6
June Medical Serv. v. Russo	Feb. 2020	15	30
Our Lady of Guadalupe v. Morrissey-Berru	*May 2020*	*15*	*9*
Trump v. New York	Dec. 2020	15	3
Biden v. Texas	Apr. 2022	15	3
Barr, Atty Gen v. AAPC Inc.	*May 2020*	*14*	*0*
Kelly v. United States	Jan. 2020	13	3
Babb v. Wilkie, Sec. of VA	Jan. 2020	13	0
McGirt v. Oklahoma	*May 2020*	*13*	*1*
United States v. Zubaydah	Oct. 2021	13	4
Carson v. Makin	Dec. 2021	13	3
DHS v. Regents of Univ. of California	Nov. 2019	12	8
Espinoza v. Montana Dept. of Revenue	Jan. 2020	12	11
Brnovich v. DNC, AZ Rep. Party v. DNC	Feb. 2021	12	0
Mahanoy Area School Dist. v. B.L.	Apr. 2021	12	5
Whole Woman's Health v. Jackson	Nov. 2021	12	3
United States v. Texas	Nov. 2021	12	2
NY State Rifle and Pistol Assn. v. Bruen	Nov. 2021	12	0
NY State Rifle & Pistol Assn., Inc. v. NYC	Dec. 2019	11	4

Two of the highest salience cases in our sample, *Kennedy v. Bremerton School Dist.* (2022), a major First Amendment case about school prayer, and *Dobbs v. Jackson Women's Health Org.* (2022), the case that overturned *Roe v. Wade* (1973), do not even make it into the top four most covered cases in our sample—although they are soundly in the top ten. The former is of moderate to low salience based on our measure of pre-argument coverage (five newspaper articles discussing it appeared prior to the day of argument) while online print media outlets published nineteen articles about it on the day it was argued. On the other hand, *Dobbs* earned the second highest salience score in the sample (twenty-eight newspaper articles that discussed it appeared prior to argument day) while it, too, enjoyed nineteen articles on its argument day. This is, perhaps, surprising as, by any account, *Dobbs* is widely considered one of the most important cases in the past several decades.

Of the remaining top ten most salient cases in the sample, only two were argued during the inaugural livestreaming session. *Trump v. Mazars* (2020)—the case involving whether the House of Representatives has the power to issue subpoenas to obtain documents from the president's private business—is third in salience and had twenty-six stories in online print media sources. Further, *Our Lady of Guadalupe v. Morrissey-Berru* (2020)—which focused on whether employees of religious organizations can bring discrimination suits against their employers—is seventh in salience and garnered fifteen online print articles published about it on argument day. The remaining top ten most salient cases were not argued during May 2020; three were argued earlier in the 2019 Term and two were argued during the October 2021 Term.

The descriptive analysis of specific case coverage certainly supports the findings from table 2.1. That is, case salience is not the only factor that contributes to increased levels of case coverage by online print outlets. Rather, the picture that emerges is that the novelty of the May 2020 session is a major contributing factor for increased argument coverage. Yet, this finding, just as with the previous section, is preliminary.

Online Print Media Coverage by Ideology of Outlet

As a final cut at the descriptive data, we seek to determine whether online print media outlets across the ideological spectrum marched in lockstep as outlined by our hypotheses or whether news outlets from one ideological perspective responded differently to the immediate access to livestreamed oral arguments. To make this determination, we analyze the number of online print news stories produced for each oral argument session by whether they emanated from a liberal news outlet, from a conservative news outlet, or from a center news outlet as defined by the Interactive Media Bias Chart.[11]

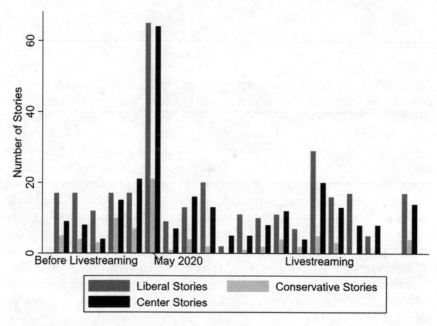

Figure 2.2　Number of Online Print Media Oral Argument Stories by Ideological Leaning of News Outlets (2019–2021 Terms). *Source:* Interactive Media Bias Chart— https://adfontesmedia.com/interactive-media-bias-chart/

Consistent with the results in figure 2.1 and table 2.1 a cursory glance at figure 2.2 indicates a similar pattern across all ideological media outlets. Indeed, online print news outlets across the ideological spectrum produced more stories during the May 2020 session than they did during any other session across our sample.[12] During this initial livestreaming session, liberal outlets produced sixty-five stories, conservative outlets produced twenty-one stories, and centrist outlets produced sixty-four stories. These increases in coverage are demarcated with the three vertical bars representing coverage of the May 2020 session. In fact, no other session came close to as much coverage within each of the three ideological groupings.

For ease of comparison, we parse out the findings for each of the ideological outlets beginning with liberal online print media. Cases argued before livestreaming produced, on average, sixteen stories per oral argument session in these outlets. Then, in May 2020, they produced a whopping sixty-five stories—just over a four-time increase in coverage. Then, when the Court reconvened with livestreaming, to begin its October 2020 term, the average dropped back to an average of eleven stories per argument session (p < 0.01 when comparing May 2020 to sessions before livestreaming and after initial livestreaming session).

The pattern is the same for conservative online print media outlets. Before livestreaming, these three outlets produced an average of just under six (5.8) stories per argument session. During the May 2020 session, this spiked to twenty-one stories. And, once the novelty of instantaneous access to arguments wore off, the average dropped below two stories (1.7) per session, on average. Finally, moderate online print media outlets are no different than their more extreme ideological partners. Prior to livestreaming they produced, on average, just over eleven articles (11.4). This average balloons to sixty-four articles during that first livestreamed session in May 2020 and then drops off to just under ten (9.5) articles per session as livestreaming continued.

Ultimately, whether we analyze the coverage of argument sessions in the aggregate, at the case level, or based on the ideological bias of a news outlet, the pattern is still the same. Indeed, media outlets acted like the general public (or at least members of the general public who are Court watchers or Court geeks) during the initial livestreamed cases in May 2020 but subsequently returned to pre-livestreaming behavior—just as life did more generally.

METHODS AND MODEL

The descriptive data in the above sections provide an interesting picture of the extent to which the Court's switch to livestreamed arguments altered the frequency of media coverage, but they do not answer the key questions of whether instant access to oral argument proceedings led, more systematically, to increased coverage of the Court's oral arguments. To make this assessment, we estimate a logistic regression model where the dependent variable (the phenomenon we seek to explain) is whether or not a *Story* appears in each of our online print news media outlets of interest about a given case in the sample.[13] In other words, for each case, the dataset contains an observation for coverage from each news outlet we examine for each case in the dataset. This yields a total of 3,132 observations.

To test our first hypothesis, *that coverage increases during the May 2020 session*, we create three variables that demarcate the *May Session*, the *Pre-May 2020 Sessions*, and the *Post-May Sessions* for oral argument. All cases within a particular time period are coded 1, and any cases outside that times-pan are coded zero. In this way we can compare how cases in each period are treated by online print media in terms of volume of coverage. For statistical purposes, we use the *Pre-May 2020* cases (that were not livestreamed) as a reference category. This means that we specifically compare the first month of livestreamed cases (May 2020) and the rest of the livestreamed cases (post-May 2020) with cases that were not livestreamed (pre-May 2020).

In addition to our two main variables of interest, we include additional variables to account for other factors that may lead to increased coverage of oral argument in a given case. Specifically, we are interested in factors that may make a case more salient and therefore more likely to be covered by the media. First, cases are often considered more salient (perhaps more contentious) when justices speak more during an oral argument (see, e.g., Black et al. 2013; Black et al. 2011). Thus, we include *Number of Turns*, which we define as the number of times each justice speaks during the arguments in a specific case. The intuition is that the more justices engage with the attorneys (and with one another) the more salient they find the case. We captured this variable by downloading every argument transcript and counting the number of times each justice spoke. We then summed individual justice utterances to obtain a total for each case.

Another way to measure salience is through media coverage, as we detail above and in chapter 1. So, we include *Pre-Argument Stories* as a measure of latent salience. As a reminder, we only count the number of articles that appear prior to the day of oral argument. Thus, this variable takes on an integer value for the number of stories from all three news outlets in Clark et al.'s (2014) data for each case in our sample.[14] The reason we include this variable is to control for the fact that online print media outlets may have been particularly interested in several key cases the justices postponed until their May 2020 session, including *Little Sisters of the Poor* (2020) and *Trump v. Vance* (2020).

Further, certain case types are considered more salient than others, in a legal sense, and may therefore generate more media coverage. As such, we include two variables from the Supreme Court Data Base (Spaeth et al. 2022) to capture such cases. A *Civil Liberties Case* is based on whether the main issue at stake relates to a civil liberties issue and *Constitutional Case* compares whether the main issue in a case involves a constitutional rather than a statutory question. Both of these variables are coded 1 if they fall into their given category and 0 if they do not. Finally, we code cases for whether the *Solicitor General* was involved in a case as a named party or *amicus curiae*.[15] The intuition is that when the office of the nation's top appellate attorney gets involved in a case it is considered more important (Black and Owens 2012) and more salient. In turn, media outlets may be more likely to provide increased coverage of it.

Table 2.2 displays the results of our model estimation. We find a statistically significant and, as we hypothesized, positive relationship between a story being published (*Story*) and our *May 2020 Session* variable.[16] What this means is that when a case was livestreamed during May 2020, its odds of having an online print news outlet reporting on it are 2.61 times greater when compared to the odds for a case that was heard when arguments were not livestreaemed.

Table 2.2   Logistic Regression of Whether Online Print News Stories Published a Story About an Orally Argued Case (2019–2021 Terms)

	Coefficient	Standard Error
May Session	2.618***	0.226
Post-May Sessions	-0.110	0.141
Number of Turns	0.014***	0.001
Pre-Argument Stories	0.167***	0.018
Civil Liberties Case	0.096	0.139
Constitutional Case	0.277*	0.124
Solicitor General	-0.192	0.127
Constant	-4.223***	0.220
Log Likelihood	-1163.510	
Number of Observations	3,132	

Note: Pre-May 2020 cases (before arguments were livestreamed) are the reference category.
*p < 0.1; **p < 0.05; ***p < 0.01, two-tailed tests.

On the other hand, we do not find a significant difference in the odds that a case is covered when comparing *Pre-May* and *Post-May Sessions*. In other words, the livestreamed cases heard after the initial May session are not significantly more likely to be covered by online print news media compared to cases that were not livestreamed. This finding holds even as we control for other possible explanations for media coverage (e.g., justices' engagement during the arguments, *Pre-Argument Stories* about the case, the type of case argued, and whether the Solicitor General was involved in the case).

We also find a significant and positive relationship between our dependent variable and several other controls: *Number of Turns*, *Pre-Argument Stories*, and *Constitutional Case*. That said, these relationships are not as strong. But they are worth noting. First, the relationship with *Pre-Argument Stories* suggests that cases covered in the media before oral argument are also more likely to have stories produced on the day of oral argument. Second for *Number of Turns*, the relationship suggests that the more times justices speak while a case is orally argued, the greater the likelihood that the oral argument in the case will be covered by the media. Finally, orally argued cases that deal with *Constitutional* issues are more likely to be covered as well.

Because results of logistic regression models are difficult to interpret, figure 2.3 provides a visualization of the relationship between our three time periods of interest—*Before Livestreaming, May 2020* arguments with livestreaming, and *Livestreaming After May 2020*—and whether our media outlets of interest published at least one article about the arguments in a case. More specifically, it demonstrates the predicted probability a story was produced about an orally argued case during the May 2020 session is roughly 0.67 while the Pre- and Post-May periods correspond to probabilities of 0.13 and 0.11 that a story was produced, respectively. This combination of findings makes it quite

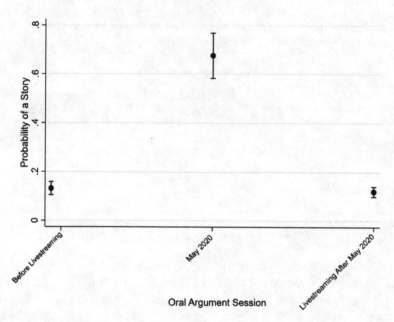

Figure 2.3 Probability That an Online Print News Story Was Published about an Orally Argued Case (2019–2021 Terms) (black dots are the point estimate, and the whiskers are the 95 percent Confidence Intervals).

clear that the media changed its coverage in May 2020, as our first hypothesis predicts. Coverage then reverted to pre-pandemic levels as livestreaming continued in October 2020. In short, we also find strong support for our second hypothesis.

CONCLUSION

We began this chapter by arguing that the first Monday in October should be a national holiday because it is the day when the nation's Court of last resort begins its annual business. Perhaps so. But what we know, for sure, is that the public treated the May 2020 argument session as a six-day celebration of the Court's arguments even though most people listened from the confines of their own homes due to the COVID-19 pandemic. In due course, however, that celebration subsided once it went beyond those six days. In other words, once the novelty of livestreaming wore off, the public and, for our purposes, the media went back to normal.

This is an important finding about how institutions react to world events—especially to major ones such as the COVID-19 pandemic. Indeed, the theory of institutional change and adaptation suggests that social, political, and legal actors can and do react when the context of the world changes. However, they also revert to their previous behavior if the institutional change becomes the new normal. Our findings add to this important multi-disciplinary literature on institutional change and adaptation.

Indeed, the empirical analysis in this chapter indicates that changes occurred in news media coverage as a result of the unprecedented access to oral argument proceedings but that these changes were limited in duration. In particular, the frequency of major news media coverage of Supreme Court oral arguments substantially increased immediately following the availability of livestreamed audio in May 2020 but this increase did not persist into the following livestreamed sessions. Rather than representing a new normal for Supreme Court coverage, the May 2020 session was a short-term disruption to the status quo. The next chapter delves even deeper into such reactions as it considers whether the actual content of coverage also changed.

Chapter 3

Did Livestreamed Arguments Change How Online Print Media Covered the Court?

INTRODUCTION

A video positioned at the top of a CNN online print news story about *Patent & Trademark v. Booking.com* (2020) included audio clips from the oral argument in the case.[1] The video begins with Chief Justice John Roberts' voice calling on Justice Clarence Thomas to indicate that, if he wanted to, Thomas could ask a question. After noting that *Booking* was the first time in history the Supreme Court had provided a live broadcast of an oral argument, the two-minute video went on to explain the logistics of oral argument procedure along with Thomas' previous pattern of listening rather than speaking during most oral arguments held in his thirty-year tenure on the bench. Then, Thomas is heard saying, "Yes, Ms. Ross. The—a couple of questions. The—could Booking acquire an 800 number, for ex—that's a vanity number, 1-800-booking, for example, that is similar to, for—1-800-plumbing, which is a registered mark?"[2] After showing text onscreen that explained and described the context for Thomas' question, Erica Ross—the then assistant to the US Solicitor General—is heard responding to Thomas, saying:

> So, Justice Thomas, under the Federal Circuit's decisions, yes, it could . . . But the core problem with Booking.com is that it allows Respondent to monopolize booking on the Internet because of the fact that longer domain names of Respondent's competitors, like ebooking.com and hotelbooking.com, can include Booking.com. That is not as obviously true of something like 1-800-booking.[3]

47

The video concludes with two more audio clips of Thomas' questioning of Ms. Ross along with some information about a case Thomas references—*Goodyear's India Rubber Glove Manufacturing Co. v. Goodyear Rubber Co.* (1888).

Was this use of oral argument audio in CNN's story about *Patent & Trademark v. Booking.com* (2020) an anomaly or the start of a new norm that would lead online print media outlets to embed direct audio from the Court's oral arguments into their stories? This question speaks to the core focus of this chapter: whether access to livestreamed oral argument audio altered the very nature of online print media coverage of these proceedings. More specifically, we examine this question by exploring *whether the media responded to immediate access to the arguments by providing more in-depth coverage of the proceedings.* As with chapter 2, we are also interested in *whether such changes in coverage continued after May 2020.*

To answer these two questions, the chapter proceeds as follows. First, we provide a brief recap of our nature of coverage argument and corresponding hypotheses. From there we analyze the descriptive data as a preliminary test of these hypotheses. We then turn to a systematic analysis of news media coverage of Supreme Court oral arguments during our period of interest. Finally, we offer some concluding remarks about what these data say about when and why the media alter coverage of this part of the justices' decision-making process.

OVERVIEW OF NATURE OF COVERAGE ARGUMENT

Chapter 2 clearly demonstrates that the volume of online print news stories, at least temporarily, increased when the Court began livestreaming its oral arguments. Beyond the increased volume of coverage, such a change to the format of these proceedings may have also altered the *nature* of news media coverage. Indeed, the availability of livestreamed audio removed barriers to in-depth reporting, which raises the possibility that news media outlets adapted to this institutional change and began covering the Court's argument sessions with much greater detail than they did when reporters had to wait hours, days, or up to a year to obtain transcripts and audio of what transpired in open court.

We anticipate the availability of livestreamed audio will alter the nature of coverage by the news media in the same way that it altered the volume of coverage. The reason is that livestreamed oral argument audio decreased the costs (e.g., time and needed resources) associated with detailed reporting on these proceedings. More specifically, livestreamed audio provides reporters with instantaneous access to these proceedings, satisfying the quick pace of the twenty-four-hour news cycle (Vasterman 2005; Ritter 2020) and reducing barriers to more in-depth coverage such as lengthier stories and the use of, close to real time, direct quotes from the proceedings. Although the Court has, for some time, released written transcripts the same day a case is heard, reporters operate on tight deadlines such that a delay of even a few hours may constrain their ability to include more quotes or other nuances from the discussions. In the twenty-four-hour news cycle environment, coverage quickly becomes old news, and the public largely loses interest in it (see, e.g., Erickson 2020).

Of course, as we noted previously, livestreamed audio was an historic development at the Court, which made it inherently a newsworthy topic. Never before had Supreme Court oral argument been available instantaneously to those outside the courtroom. The novelty of livestreaming, therefore, incentivized in-depth coverage in the short term and such detailed coverage was possible due to the ability to play back livestreamed audio prior to a media deadline. But as the novelty of livestreamed oral argument wore off, however, journalists faced pressure to move on to the next big stories (Zamith and Braun 2019; Örnebring 2018) rather than continue to cover the Court in such depth. Thus, we also anticipate that the change in media coverage is most likely short-lived.

Combined, these arguments lead us to expect that *online print media sources will increase the length of stories, the number of direct quotations, and the length of quotations for the initial May 2020 argument sessions but that these increases will not continue in the long term.*

DESCRIPTIVE DATA

In this section, we turn to data that allow us to test these hypotheses. We do so through a variety of lenses. As a first cut, we analyze which oral argument sessions in our sample garnered the most in-depth online print media coverage in terms of story length.[4] This initial measure is certainly blunt, but we take this tack because the length of story may be indicative of the media providing greater or additional detail to coverage of these proceedings.

Next, to assess the depth of coverage, we examine online print media's use of quotations from the oral argument participants. We do so in a number of ways. First, we consider separately the number of times justices and attorneys are directly quoted, as well as the extent to which quotes from individual justices and attorneys—those representing the petitioner versus the respondent—are included in oral argument coverage. Second, we turn to an examination of the cases whose online print media coverage featured the greatest number of quotes. Third, we analyze the types of quotes online print media outlets use when they embed them in articles about oral arguments.

We are especially interested in the degree to which outlets utilize snippets of quotes (i.e., just a few words or invoke ellipses to decrease the length of a quote) versus a full sentence (or multiple sentences) quotes that provide more context as to what the justice or attorney said.[5]

Beyond the use of direct quotations from oral argument sessions, we may also gain traction on how media changed coverage when livestreaming began by whether or not the media outlets in our sample offered more original reporting of oral arguments or whether they were more likely to reprint wire stories from other top, sometimes larger, outlets (e.g., *The Associated Press*, *The New York Times*, *Wall Street Journal*, and *The Washington Post*).[6]

Finally, we turn back to the example from the introduction of this chapter, examining whether or not livestreaming led online print media outlets to increase their use of embedded audio clips from the oral arguments. The intuition is that instantaneous access to the Court's audio makes it easier for outlets to use this strategy. Indeed, given the theory of the fast-paced, twenty-four-hour news cycle, such immediate access should make embedding audio clips much more likely once livestreaming began—at least in the short term—as our two hypotheses suggest.

Did Livestreaming Change the Length of News Stories about Oral Arguments?

We begin by examining the length of oral argument news stories for all sessions in our sample. In particular, figure 3.1 displays the average word count for online print news stories over this time. The apex of the line occurs during the first month of livestreamed oral arguments—May 2020.

Several findings are immediately evident. First, coverage produced during the initial month of livestreaming is by far the lengthiest, on average, in the sample. Stories during this month were an average of 599.0 words long while those published prior to and after this session averaged 158.0 and 128.2 words long respectively ($p < 0.05$ for both comparisons—before livestreaming and for all cases during the October 2020 and 2021 Terms). To put it another way, this media output is more than three times the average for pre-livestreamed (October 2019 Term) sessions and more than four times the average for the rest of the livestreamed sessions (October 2020 and 2021 Terms).

Individual media outlets mirror the aggregate finding in this figure. During the May 2020 session, *The New York Times*, *The Washington Post*, and CNN produced the longest stories about arguments, averaging 891.1 words (897.3, 930.0, and 846.0, respectively). On the other hand, smaller news outlets such as the *New York Post* and *Newsday* reported about the Court with an average of only 168.5 words per story during the May 2020 session (188.0 and 149.0,

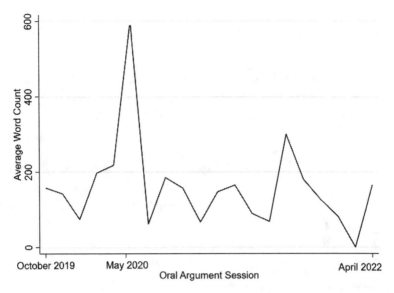

Figure 3.1   Average Word Count of Online Print News Stories about Orally Argued Cases (2019–2021 Terms).

respectively). Despite the smaller averages for these outlets, those with permanent press credentials for the Court (the *Times*, *Post*, and CNN) all quite clearly parallel the aggregate findings.

Second, the visual trend in figure 3.1 shows that the length of news stories written about oral arguments before livestreaming and after the first month of this new procedure strongly resembles one another. In more concrete terms, none of the stories prior to, or after, May 2020 were more than 300 words long, on average. Put another way, online print news coverage of arguments reverted back to normal after the overwhelming focus on these proceedings during the May 2020 livestreamed sessions. In terms of our hypotheses, while the length of coverage increased for the first month of livestreaming, we observe the same overall trend as with the frequency of coverage. In short, the shift to lengthier coverage by online print media outlets during May 2020 was temporary. Take *The New York Times*, for example. It published sixteen stories during the May 2020 session with an average of 897.3 words. Before livestreaming, the average word count for its articles about Supreme Court oral arguments was roughly 450.8 words and after livestreaming (excluding May 2020) the average dropped back to 335.8 words.

Collectively, these data provide strong support for our hypothesis and suggest that, after a major increase in coverage surrounding the first month of livestreaming, the media reverted back pre-livestreaming norms of coverage about oral arguments. In short, just as in chapter 2, the media responded to the novelty of the transition to livestreaming but, as with all institutions, adapted to the change by October 2020.

Did Livestreaming Change How Online Print Media Used Quotations from Oral Arguments?

We next assess whether the propensity of online print media to incorporate into their stories quotes of justices' questions or comments made during oral argument—as opposed to summarizing what occurred during the proceedings—increased when the Court began livestreaming. This is an important indicator of increased depth of coverage because incorporating quotes allows reporters to enhance coverage with salient and important aspects of the dialogue between the Court and counsel. Empirically, it is clear that quotes are commonly used within the text of online print media stories as 3,586 quotes from justices or advocates appear across our sample of 644 news articles.

Examining the use of quotations provides another lens through which we can assess whether the nature of news media coverage of oral arguments changed when the Court began livestreaming and whether these potential changes continued in the coverage of cases argued after the May 2020 session. To do so, we first consider whether the number of quotes used—from justices and then attorneys—shifted over the sessions in our sample. From there we investigate the types of quotes used. As we point out above, we specifically compare the use of full-sentence (or more) quotes versus shorter quotes. Finally, we assess the extent to which oral argument audio clips—a way to quote justices and attorneys made possible by livestreaming—are embedded in online print stories. Once again, the evidence generally indicates that livestreaming led to more in-depth coverage but that this change did not persist in online print media coverage in the long term.

Use of Direct Justice Quotations from Oral Arguments

Figure 3.2 displays the average number of times any justice is quoted in the text of online print news media articles across our twenty argument sessions of interest. The black bar denotes the shift to livestreamed audio in May 2020. The results are strikingly similar to those in figure 3.1 and to the volume of coverage data in chapter 2. Specifically, justices are quoted an average of 13.1 times per oral argument session before COVID-19 led the Court to livestream its proceedings. This average climbs to 54.2 quotes per session during the initial month of livestreaming. From there, as we expected, the average dips back to 10.1 times per session during the remainder of the livestreamed sessions in the 2020 and 2021 Terms ($p < 0.05$ for both before livestreaming

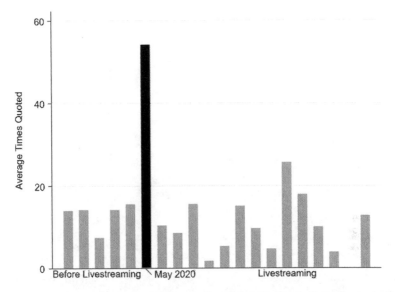

Figure 3.2 Average Number of Times Online Print Media Outlets Quote Justices (2019–2021 Terms).

and after livestreaming when compared to the May 2020 session). Overall, while there is variation in the use of quotes in online print media outlets, this variation does not appear to be shaped, in the long run, by the availability of livestreamed oral argument audio—as our hypothesis predicts.

We are also interested in the frequency of online print news media outlets utilizing quotes of specific justices since the aggregate trend may mask individual-level variation. Figures 3.3a and 3.3b display the total number of times each justice was quoted by the media across the sessions in our sample.[7] While variation exists in the propensity of media outlets to quote a given justice, there is not an overall sustained increase in the use of quotes, once livestreaming began, for individual justices.

The exception, of course, is Thomas. His increased participation in oral argument—widely attributed to the change in procedure that gave each justice a dedicated opportunity to pose questions without having to interrupt their colleagues' questions (Johnson et al. 2021)—was a significant departure from his previous norm of mostly listening, rather than posing questions, during these proceedings. In fact, his change in behavior drew widespread attention from the media and Court scholars alike (see, e.g., Johnson et al. 2021; Jacobi et al. 2021; Ringsmuth et al. 2023).

Despite the variation depicted for each justice, figures 3.3a and 3.3b demonstrate support for our hypothesis that online print media outlets used more

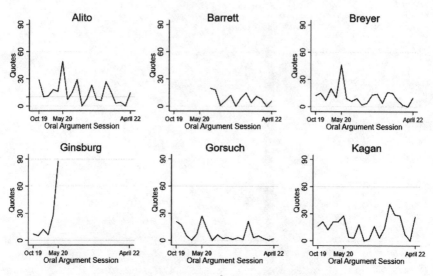

Figure 3.3a   Number of Individual Justice Quotes Used by Online Print Media Outlets (2019–2021 Terms).

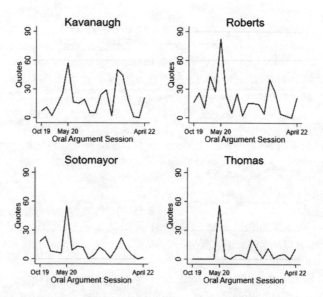

Figure 3.3b   Number of Individual Justice Quotes Used by Online Print Media Outlets (2019–2021 Terms).

justice quotes during May 2020 compared to the sessions that occurred before livestreaming. Even when we account for the number of stories produced during each oral argument session, this finding holds for all justices with the exception of Kagan. Across all twenty sessions in our dataset, Roberts is quoted most frequently—401 times—in news stories about oral argument. This supports the research that the chief justice tends to speak the most at oral argument (Johnson and Gregory 2016). Following Roberts are Justice Brett Kavanaugh (n = 364), Justice Elena Kagan (n = 311), and then Justice Samuel Alito (n = 293).

The media's use of quotes from Justice Stephen Breyer during the March 2020 and May 2020 sessions illustrates the overarching pattern in how he and his colleagues were quoted by online print media outlets. In March of 2020, right before livestreaming, Breyer was quoted ten times across forty-five stories. This means that, on average, he was quoted 0.22 times per story. In May 2020, there were 150 stories produced and 46 of them contained a quote from Breyer. This means, on average, he was quoted 0.31 times per story. These data suggest Breyer was quoted roughly 41 percent more in May 2020 compared to stories written right before livestreaming began.

Table 3.1 also provides additional support for our two main hypotheses. It depicts the twenty-five cases in our dataset whose coverage contains the greatest number of direct quotes from the justices. Cases argued in May 2020, when audio livestreaming began, are disproportionately represented on the list with all ten of the cases argued featuring a high number of quotes in news media coverage.[8] No other month of oral argument sittings had every one of its cases make it into this top twenty-five list.[9]

The top three cases, *Trump v. Mazars* (2020), *Patent & Trademark v. Booking.com* (2020), and *Chiafalo* (2020), all emanate from the May 2020 argument session, as indicated by bold italics. They garner fifteen, thirteen, and thirteen quotes, respectively. Two other cases from the initial month of livestreaming also garner more than ten justices quotes in the articles published about their oral arguments: *Little Sisters of the Poor v. Pennsylvania* (2020) and *Our Lady of Guadalupe v. Morrissey-Berru* (2020). Finally, *Barr v. American Assn. of Political Consultants, Inc.* (2020), *McGirt v. Oklahoma* (2020), and *USAID v. Alliance for Open Society International, Inc.* (2020) have nine, nine, and eight direct justices quotes in their oral argument coverage, respectively.

These findings are even more notable given that some of the cases from May 2020 did not receive much media coverage prior to oral argument (see chapter 1 and chapter 2 for additional discussion of this measure of salience that we call *Pre-Argument Stories*). For instance, the case in our sample that had garnered the most coverage prior to its argument day (twenty-eight stories), *Dobbs v. Jackson Women's Health Org.* (2022), quoted justices' questions or comments thirteen times from the arguments. This is the same

Table 3.1 Top Twenty-Five Cases with the Most Justice Quotes in Online Print News Stories (2019–2021 Terms)

Case Name	OA Session	Number of Quotes	Pre-Argument Stories
Trump v. Mazars/ Trump v. Vance	*May 2020*	*15*	*23*
Patent & Trademark v. Booking.com	*May 2020*	*13*	*3*
Chiafalo v. Washington	*May 2020*	*13*	*4*
Dobbs v. Jackson Women's Health Org.	Dec. 2021	13	28
June Medical Serv. v. Russo	Feb. 2020	12	30
Little Sisters of the Poor v. Pennsylvania	*May 2020*	*12*	*2*
Carson v. Makin	Dec. 2021	12	3
Kelly v. United States	Jan. 2020	11	3
Our Lady of Guadalupe v. Morrissey-Berru	*May 2020*	*11*	*9*
United States v. Zubaydah	Oct. 2021	11	4
Whole Woman's Health v. Jackson	Nov. 2021	11	3
Biden v. Texas	Apr. 2022	11	3
Trump v. New York	Dec. 2020	10	3
United States v. Texas	Nov. 2021	10	2
FEC v. Ted Cruz for Senate	Jan. 2022	10	2
Babb v. Wilkie, Sec. of VA	Jan. 2020	9	0
Espinoza v. Montana Dept. of Revenue	Jan. 2020	9	11
Seila Law LLC v. Consumer Protection Bureau	Feb. 2020	9	6
Barr, Atty Gen v. AAPC, Inc.	*May 2020*	*9*	*0*
McGirt v. Oklahoma	*May 2020*	*9*	*1*
Brnovich v. DNC, AZ Republican Party v. DNC	Feb. 2021	9	0
New York State Rifle and Pistol Assn. v. Bruen	Nov. 2021	9	0
Kennedy v. Bremerton School Dist.	Apr. 2022	9	5
NY State Rifle & Pistol Assn., Inc. v. NYC	Dec. 2019	8	4
USAID v. AFOSI, Inc.	*May 2020*	*8*	*0*

number of justice quotes as were used from a May 2020 case, *Patent & Trademark v. Booking.com* (2020), which had only three stories written about it prior to the argument day. *Chiafalo v. Washington* (2020) provides another example; it had only four stories published about it prior to arguments and yet it is the case with the third most justice quotes in table 3.1.

Again, the evidence indicates the use of justice quotations from oral arguments in online print media coverage is not necessarily driven by case salience in the short term but, rather, by the novelty associated with the first month of livestreaming. This is another piece of the puzzle that, as we place them all together, supports the hypotheses we explicated in the Introduction.

Use of Direct Attorney Quotations from Oral Arguments

The media are not only interested in quoting justices' questions and comments. As such, we also examine quotes the media used from attorneys during argument. Figure 3.4 displays the same trend as the media's use of justices' quotations. Across all our sessions of interest, petitioner and respondent attorneys were quoted 686 and 562 times, respectively. During the May 2020 session, however, both sets of attorneys were quoted the most. For petitioner attorneys (represented by the black line) the average number of times they were quoted in a session is 31.4 times. However, in May 2020 this spiked to 101.0 quotations and then decreased to an average of 32.9 thereafter. The same story holds for respondent attorneys (represented by the gray line). Online print outlets, on average, quoted respondent attorneys an average of 31.4 times before livestreaming. Then, in May 2020 they quoted respondents 77.0 times, only to dip back down to an average of 25.2 during the remaining livestreamed sessions during the October 2020 and 2021 Terms.

Across the media's use of justice and attorney quotations in the text of online print stories, the sessions after the first month of livestreaming offer support for our second hypothesis that the considerable increase in media use of quotes from oral argument is connected to the novelty of livestreaming these proceedings. Indeed, the combination of the quantitative and qualitative evidence suggests that, despite the availability of instantaneous source information, reporters reverted to their old form of content that included fewer quotes and more general case summaries in the long term.

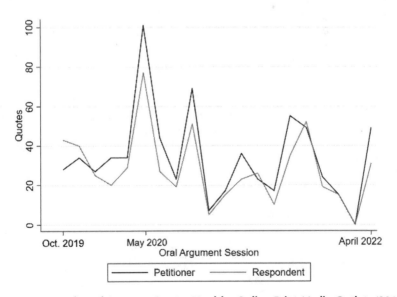

Figure 3.4   Number of Attorney Quotes Used by Online Print Media Outlets (2019–2021 Terms).

In short, as with all institutions they adapted to their new reality of livestreamed arguments.

Length of Justice Quotations from Oral Arguments

Beyond the general use of quotes from justices and attorneys, it is also possible that having audio immediately available to reporters covering the Court changed the length of justice quotes used in stories. This is an important point to consider because former and current justices have expressed concern about the potential for journalists to take their words out of context if the media's access to oral argument proceedings was increased, for example, to allow video cameras (Carter 2012; Mauro 2011). In our phenomenon of interest, the ability to play back argument audio reduced barriers to including longer quotes in stories about oral argument, which could impact the portrayal of the Court to the public.

To assess whether livestreamed audio produced shorter, sound bite-type, quotes from the justices' questions or comments, we coded each justice quote contained in each news story in our dataset. We labeled quotes based on whether the news outlet quoted at least a full sentence from a justice or whether the outlet took snippets—less than a full sentence—from a longer quote. For example, in *The Washington Post* coverage of *Sanchez v. Mayorkas, Sec. of Homeland Security* (2021), they said Breyer claimed, "it was possible the government was being generous in extending temporary protection—but that 'temporary' was the operative term." In this excerpt, the word "temporary" is a snippet from Breyer's comment. On the other hand, *The Post* quoted a complete sentence from Roberts who, when speaking to the government's attorney said, "I was struck by the extent to which your brief undersold your position."

Figure 3.5 depicts the percentage of justice quotes used in media accounts that are a full sentence or longer across all sessions in the sample. Because justice quotes are coded as either at least one sentence long or not, an increase in the number of full-sentence quotes necessarily corresponds to a decrease in the number of snippet quotes. The y-axis lists each oral argument session in our sample. The black bar depicts the first month of livestreaming.

The figure indicates that livestreaming oral argument audio did not affect the propensity for media outlets to utilize more full-sentence quotes from the justices. Before livestreaming, on average, media outlets quoted justices using at least one full sentence about 72 percent of the time, which means that 28 percent of the time they used snippets. The proportion of full-sentence

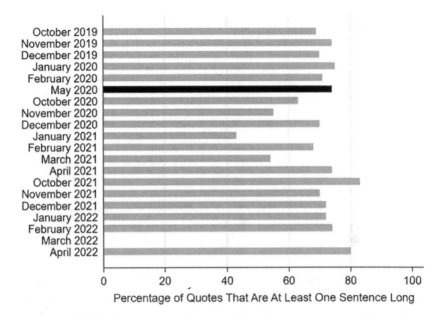

Figure 3.5 Percentage of Justice or Advocate Quotes That Are at Least One Full Sentence in Online Print News Stories (2019–2021 Terms).

quotes increases to seventy-four during the May 2020 session and then dips slightly to 68 percent for the remaining sessions but the difference does not reach the conventional level of statistical significance ($p > 0.05$ for all comparisons). These are the first data that do not comport with our hypothesis that coverage would change during the May 2020 session. However, because reporters are still pressed for time, it is possible they wanted to use more full-sentence quotes but settled for more quotes overall. Importantly, though, the evidence about the length of quotes indicates that livestreaming did not alter the nature of online print media coverage in the long term, echoing earlier findings.

To further explore whether online print media's use of justice quotes from oral argument changed after the advent of livestreaming, we break down how often each individual justice is quoted using a full sentence (or longer). As table 3.2 shows, all justices are quoted quite often using at least one sentence: between 55.8 percent and 82.9 percent of the time. Justice Neil Gorsuch is quoted the least often using one or more sentences, which means that roughly half the time news outlets use snippets of Gorsuch's oral argument engagement. Justice Ruth Bader Ginsburg was quoted the most often using at least one full sentence (82.9 percent).

Table 3.2 Percentage of Justice or Advocate Quotes That Are at Least One Full Sentence in Online Print News Stories (2019–2021 Terms)

Speaker	Sessions before Livestreaming (%)	May 2020 Session (%)	Sessions after Livestreaming (Post-May 2020) (%)	Across All Sessions (%)
Alito	69.96	53.06	73.12	69.96
Barrett	N/A	N/A	68.18	68.18
Breyer	73.75	76.08	72.07	73.75
Ginsburg	82.87	85.22	N/A	82.87
Gorsuch	55.79	62.96	55.73	55.79
Kagan	72.66	78.57	69.79	72.66
Kavanaugh	82.85	63.15	62.24	63.45
Roberts	72.81	74.39	74.11	72.81
Sotomayor	79.46	81.81	77.57	79.46
Thomas	70.76	82.14	62.16	70.76
Petitioner	58.59	62.37	59.81	59.91
Respondent	67.51	66.23	55.4	60.32

Following Ginsburg is Justice Sonia Sotomayor who, on average, is quoted 79.5 percent of the time with at least one full sentence.

It turns out that, in the May 2020 session, many of the justices were more likely to be quoted using at least one sentence or more, which is more than they were quoted in this manner during previous or subsequent sessions. Gorsuch, for instance, increased from 55.8 percent to 63.0 percent and Thomas increased from 70.8 percent before livestreaming to 82.1 percent during the May session. In contrast, some justices were less likely to be quoted using at least one sentence during the May session. For example, Alito decreased from 70.0 percent down to 53.1 percent.

While two justices experienced an increase in the proportion of "snippet" quotes in news media coverage over the long term—Kavanaugh and Thomas—we do not, on the whole, find systematic evidence of a change in whether online print media used full-sentence quotes versus snippets before May 2020 or in the months after livestreaming began.

Finally, as a normative note, figure 3.5 reveals that it is most common for justice quotes to be at least one sentence or longer compared to partial sentence snippets in online print news media coverage. While a single sentence could still be taken out of context, this finding indicates that reporters generally try to contextualize justices' participation in oral argument by quoting more fully than a few words or even a phrase. This could possibly allay the justices' concerns about placing cameras in the courtroom. We return to this point in our conclusion.

Length of Attorney Quotations from Oral Arguments

While we only offer a glimpse of the data here, the results for petitioner and respondent attorney quotes are similar to what we found for justices. Before livestreaming, petitioner attorneys were quoted roughly 58 percent of the time using at least one full sentence. This bumps up to 62 percent during the May session and then drops back very slightly to 59 percent for the remainder of the sessions. For respondent attorneys, there is less than a percentage point difference between the pre-livestreaming sessions and the May session. However, they are quoted using at least a full sentence much less after this initial May session—dropping from 66 percent to 55 percent. While it is unclear what may have caused this drop, it does not appear to be a direct effect of livestreaming since it occurred after the initial month when this newfound access was provided to the media and public alike. Ultimately, the evidence we present here combines to indicate that questions or comments from both justices and attorneys during livestreamed oral arguments were not used differently in the long term than they were prior to livestreaming.

Did Livestreaming Lead to Less Original Reporting?

Next, we turn to the degree to which all online print media outlets run original stories versus reprinting them from other sources.[10] We consider this cut at the data because our main hypothesis leads us to expect that the novelty of the initial change to livestreaming would motivate outlets to get in on the action and report about the Court's arguments. However, many smaller outlets such as the *Boston Globe*, *New York Post*, and *Newsday* do not frequently cover Supreme Court oral arguments and are therefore not well positioned to do so independently—even when a newsworthy development occurs.

While it would be ideal for these outlets to produce their own stories about arguments, we expect that resources often preclude original reporting and that they will instead rely more heavily on newswires for coverage, reprinting stories from sources such as the *Associated Press*.[11] Once the novelty faded and livestreaming seemed to become the new normal, we anticipate that these outlets will revert to previous norms and pick up fewer newswire stories about the Court's arguments. Figure 3.6 displays our data to test this proposition— the percentage of original versus reprinted stories from each argument session.

We find that the proportion of online print stories that are written as original articles decreases when the Court transitioned to livestreamed arguments. However, parallel to the above findings, this change is only

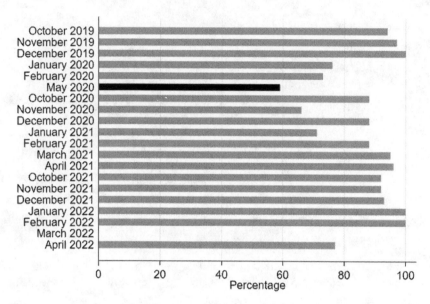

Figure 3.6   Percentage of Online Print Media Stories That Are Original (2019–2021 Terms).

temporary. Before livestreaming, media outlets, on average, produced 88 percent original stories—meaning online print news outlets took about 12 percent of their stories from the newswire. During the May 2020 session, this dropped to 59 percent and quickly spiked right back up after the initial livestreaming session. Across the sessions after May 2020, the average is, again, 88 percent. The differences between the May 2020 session and the pre-livestreaming and post-livestreaming sessions are statistically significant ($p < 0.05$). Since chapter 2 showed an increase in the number of stories overall during the May 2020 session, the temporary dip in the proportion of online print coverage that is original indicates some outlets were following the hype around the new transition to livestreaming but did not have the resources to write their own stories.[12] Instead, they relied more heavily on the wire.

Use of Oral Argument Audio Clips

We finally turn back to where we began this chapter—coverage of *Patent & Trademark v. Booking.com* (2020). Coverage of this case illustrates that outlets occasionally embed audio clips from oral argument into online print stories. This practice was made possible because of the Court's transition to livestreaming. Prior to May 2020, audio was not available in time to meet media deadlines. Indeed, as we note in the Introduction, audio was usually released at the end of each argument week. Thus, any instance of an embedded audio clip in an online print story represents a new phenomenon—a new way to employ oral argument quotes—that emerged in May of 2020. The important question for us is whether such clips became a new norm for online print coverage of oral argument. The short answer is no. While our data indicate that audio clips exist in the months after livestreaming began, in the long term they occur only rarely.

To assess the potential use of audio clips in online print coverage, we coded whether each story included *any* instance of oral argument audio. We coded very inclusively, counting a story as having an audio clip regardless of the length of time a justice or advocate spoke within the clip. Figure 3.7 displays the number of stories with at least one audio clip from oral argument. As with the previous figures, the black bar denotes the advent of livestreaming in May 2020. We note three key takeaways from these data.

First, as was the case for both the number of justice and attorney quotes used in text, the number of audio clips increased temporarily during the initial month of livestreaming. Eight out of the ten cases from this session had an audio clip embedded in coverage of them. Further, twenty-three stories in the May 2020 session featured audio clips. Early audio clips highlighted the historic nature

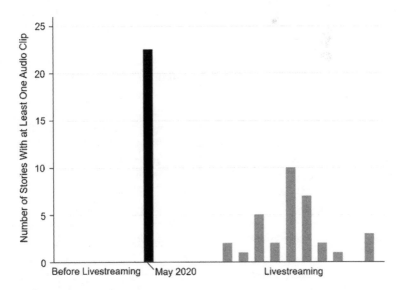

Figure 3.7 Number of Online Print Media Stories with at Least One Embedded Audio Clip (2019–2021 Terms).

of livestreaming and tended to feature Marshal Pamela Talkin, saying "Oyez, oyez, oyez" as she called the Court to order and the chief justice as he began arguments by introducing the case by name and docket number. The case whose coverage was most likely to feature audio form oral argument (nine stories total)—*Trump v. Mazars* (2020)—was argued in May 2020 and was also the case whose coverage was most likely to include justice quotes in the text of the story. Thus, media outlets' use of audio clips paralleled their use of quotations more generally, albeit at a lower overall rate.

Second, the number of stories with embedded oral argument audio decreased substantially after the novel and historic first month of livestreaming ended. Indeed, no audio clips were used in stories for the next four sessions. Beginning with the February 2021 session, however, outlets again began to incorporate audio clips into a handful of stories. From this point, through the end of the timespan we examine (April 2022), an average of thirty-four stories featured audio clips—a substantial contrast to the twenty-three stories with audio in the May 2020 session alone. The session with the next most stories featuring audio clips was November of 2021. Here clips from five cases—*Whole Woman's Health v. Jackson* (2021), *United States v. Texas* (2021), *New York State Rifle and Pistol Assn. v. Bruen* (2022), *FBI v. Fazaga* (2022), and *Ramirez v. Collier* (2022)—were used in a combined total of ten stories. The decrease in audio clip usage is further evidenced by the fact that these five cases, combined, garnered only one more story with an audio clip (ten stories) compared to *Trump v. Mazars* (2020) (nine stories)—the case heard in May of 2020. Similarly, the case with the most stories using oral argument audio clips after the first month of livestreaming—*Dobbs v. Jackson Women's Health Org.* (2022), which would ultimately overturn *Roe v. Wade* (1973)—had only six stories containing audio clips despite its widespread salience for the public and the press alike.

Third, and most importantly, the number of stories with at least one audio clip constitutes a small fraction of oral argument coverage. Indeed, for arguably the most publicly recognizable case in our dataset, *Dobbs v. Jackson Women's Health Org.* (2022)—heard during the December 2021 session—only 31.5 percent of stories featured at least one audio clip. As the case with the highest proportion of online print stories that feature at least one audio clip, *Dobbs* represents one end of the spectrum. In contrast, during the May 2020 session, only 15.3 percent of stories in our dataset contained an audio clip from oral argument, and in the months after May 2020, only 10.4 percent of stories overall included audio from oral argument.

In sum, while livestreamed oral argument has opened the door to embedding audio clips within stories, this practice is the exception not the rule. Indeed, online print outlets eschewed clips from oral argument in roughly 89 percent of stories published after livestreaming began, including May

2020. We observe a similar pattern for audio clips compared to that of the depth of oral argument coverage by online print outlets more generally. That is, there was a temporary increase when the novelty of livestreaming was high during the initial May 2020 session, but this substantial increase was not sustained over the long term. Importantly, the use of audio clips does not fully return to zero—its pre-livestreaming norm—but such coverage is rare.

METHODS AND MODEL

The descriptive evidence thus far suggests that reporters absolutely reacted when the Court began livestreaming arguments in May 2020 but that they went back to their normal coverage of oral arguments after those ten initial cases (i.e., in the October 2020 and October 2021 Terms). However, these data do not answer the key questions of whether this change led to a fundamentally different type of coverage and, if it did, what led to such a change. To make this determination we now turn to a more systematic assessment of quotes used in stories about these proceedings by modeling the extent to which access to livestreamed audio influences the likelihood that a given story contains at least one *Justice Quote* in it. Because the variable is dichotomous (1 if a story contains a quote and 0 otherwise), we again estimate a logistic regression model.

To test our first hypothesis, *that justice quotes are more prominent during the May 2020 Session*, we create three variables that demarcate the *May Session*, the *Pre-May 2020 Sessions*, and the *Post-May Sessions* for oral argument. All cases within a particular timespan are coded 1 and any cases outside that period are coded zero. In this way we can compare how cases in each time period are treated by online print media in terms of volume of quotes. For statistical purposes, we use the *Pre-May 2020* cases (that were not livestreamed) as a reference category. This means that we specifically compare the first month of livestreamed cases (May 2020) and the rest of the livestreamed cases (post-May 2020) with cases that were not livestreamed (pre-May 2020).[13]

As in chapter 2, in addition to our main variables of interest, we include variables to account for other factors that may have increased the likelihood of online print media to use more quotes from a given case. First, cases are often considered more contentious or salient when justices speak more during an oral argument. Thus, we include *Number of Turns*, which measures the number of times each justice speaks during the arguments in a specific case (see, e.g., Black et al. 2013; Black et al. 2011). We captured this variable by downloading every argument transcript and counting the number of times each justice spoke. We then summed individual justice utterances to obtain a total for each case.

Second, as we discussed in chapter 1 and above in this chapter, we include a measure of *Pre-Argument Stories*. We use the number of articles that appear prior to the day of oral argument. Thus, this variable takes on an integer value for the number of pre-oral argument stories from all three news outlets in Clark et al.'s data for each case. This allows us to distinguish between the level of media attention garnered by a given case itself as opposed to the novelty of livestreaming during the May 2020 session.

Finally, certain case types are considered more controversial than others and may therefore generate more media coverage. As such, we include two variables from the Supreme Court Data Base (Spaeth et al. 2022) to capture these cases. *Civil Liberties Case* is based on whether the main issue of a case falls in this category (coded 1) or not (coded 0) and *Constitutional Case* compares whether the case involves a constitutional rather than a statutory issue. Both are coded 1 if they fall into the category and 0 if they do not. Next, we code cases for whether the *Solicitor General* was involved as a party in a case or as *amicus curiae*. The intuition is that when the office for the nation's top appellate attorney gets involved in a case it is considered more important (Black and Owens 2012) and, in turn, may therefore be more likely to garner increased media coverage.

The results are displayed in table 3.3. They reinforce the descriptive finding that May 2020 arguments were treated fundamentally differently, in terms of coverage, than were cases argued prior to that month but that the media returned to its normal coverage when the Court reconvened for its October 2020 session. In addition, stories are more likely to include at least one quote from oral arguments as the number of justices' speaking turns during these proceedings increase and in cases that received higher levels of pre-oral

Table 3.3 Logistic Regression of Whether Online Print News Stories Include at Least One Justice Quotation from an Orally Argued Case (2019–2021 Terms)

	Coefficient	Standard Error
May 2020 Session	2.393***	0.217
After Livestreaming Sessions	-0.283	0.147
Number of Turns	0.013***	0.001
Pre-Argument Stories	0.109***	0.013
Civil Liberties Case	0.222	0.145
Constitutional Case	0.209	0.135
Solicitor General	-0.267*	0.143
Constant	-4.184***	0.234
Log Likelihood	-1045.025	
Number of Observations	3132	

Note: Pre-May 2020 cases (before arguments were livestreamed) are the reference category.
*p < 0.1; **p < 0.05; ***p < 0.01, two-tailed tests.

argument coverage—both of which serve as indicators of case salience and therefore newsworthiness. Somewhat surprisingly, cases in which the Solicitor General is involved are associated with a decreased likelihood of including a quote from a justice in an online print news article.

Because the results of logistic regression models are difficult to interpret, figure 3.8 provides a visualization of the relationship between our three sessions of interest—*Before Livestreaming* arguments, *May 2020* arguments, and *Livestreaming After May 2020* arguments—and whether a media outlet uses at least one quote from a justice in a story about a given oral argument. More specifically, it demonstrates the predicted probability at least one quote was used in a story about an orally argued case during the May 2020 session is roughly 58 percent while before livestreaming and after May 2020 sessions correspond to an 11 percent and 8 percent predicted probability a quote was used, respectively. This combination of probabilities makes it quite clear that online print media changed how it covered oral argument in May 2020—as our first hypothesis predicts—but went back to normal coverage as livestreaming continued in October 2020. In short, we also find strong support for our second hypothesis.

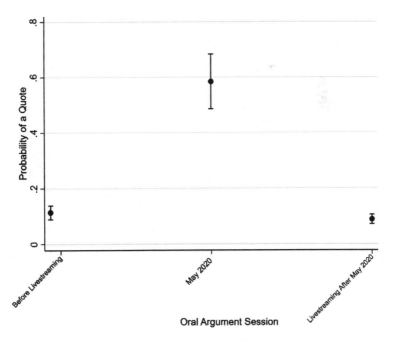

Figure 3.8   Probability That an Online Print News Story Contains at Least One Justice Quote (2019–2021 Terms) (black dots are the point estimate and the whiskers are the 95 percent Confidence Intervals).

CONCLUSION

In this chapter, we investigated whether livestreaming oral argument audio changed the nature of the online print news media's coverage of the Supreme Court. The evidence indicates, as our first hypothesis predicts, that *the nature of online print media coverage changed dramatically during the May 2020 argument session.* However, consistent with our second hypothesis, such coverage *did not change in the long term.* In other words, while livestreaming removed, or at least reduced, significant barriers to more in-depth coverage of the Court, the length of stories and the use of quotes by online print news media in the months after the Court began livestreaming looked very much like the coverage before livestreaming. The one exception is the new practice of occasionally embedding audio clips from oral argument into online print stories. While this is a change to the nature of coverage, it occurs in only a small minority of stories about oral argument.

If greater access to oral argument proceedings changed the news coverage the public relies on to be informed about the Supreme Court, this could serve as a warning about the risks to the Court's legitimacy. Instead, the consistency in the content of coverage we observe—how oral argument quotes are used and the depth of news media coverage—suggests that the increased access that livestreaming provides for the news media and the public does not come at a significant cost to the Court. The pressures of the twenty-four-hour news cycle likely constrain the extent to which news media outlets increase scrutiny of a single institution or entity such as the Court, even when access increases. While a tipping point may exist, the evidence suggests that there is room for the Supreme Court to move closer to the democratic ideal of transparency in government institutions.

In the next chapter, we turn our attention to broadcast coverage of oral arguments. We examine whether our findings for online print media—short-term changes but long-term stability in the frequency and nature of news coverage—extend to broadcast outlets.

Chapter 4

Did Livestreamed Arguments Change the Volume and Content of Broadcast Media Coverage?

INTRODUCTION

The coronavirus pandemic altered how people engaged with the world, including how Americans spent their time. Perhaps most distinctively, the share of employed Americans working from home nearly doubled during the pandemic, rising to 42 percent.[1] As more Americans began working remotely, they began to engage in more leisure activities throughout their days, consuming unprecedented levels of media to keep entertained while staying safe indoors. After sleeping, at the peak of the pandemic, the US Bureau of Labor Statistics estimates that people spent about three hours per day watching television—time spent on a sofa that may have otherwise been spent perusing malls or attending live events like concerts.[2] In short, more than ever, Americans became a nation of couch potatoes.

Media consumption—specifically television consumption for our purposes—spiked in the early days of the pandemic as Americans actively sought information and entertainment while at home. In this chapter, we seek to understand whether a trend similar to what we found in chapters 2 and 3 exists between media outlets and their broadcast, or television, coverage of oral arguments. That is, we ask, *did broadcast media coverage of the Supreme Court's oral arguments spike in the early days of livestreaming? And, if so, did this spike persist and for how long?* To answer these questions, we explore trends in our original dataset but focus here on broadcast coverage over the three-year period in our sample.

As was the case for online print outlets, broadcast news outlets previously faced both the constraints imposed by the Court's policy regarding the delayed release of oral argument transcripts and audio recordings and the pressure associated with the twenty-four-hour news cycle to quickly cover emerging stories (Vasterman 2005; Ritter 2020). The advent of livestreamed oral argument proceedings was novel and also increased access to the primary source material, which decreased barriers to providing timely and in-depth coverage for reporters. However, the inherent newsworthiness of a given case remains unchanged by livestreaming. Thus, we again expect that news outlets will alter their coverage in response to immediate access to oral arguments via livestreaming but that coverage in the long term will not substantially change.

To assess these expectations, we examine the volume and nature of broadcast news coverage of oral arguments. As to the former, we explore aggregate coverage, coverage by individual media outlets, and coverage of ideologically distinct media outlets. Then, we turn to the nature of such coverage to determine how broadcast outlets discussed arguments. Next, we take a detour to examine a related issue—common trends in broadcast coverage. Finally, we consider mentions of the Court's transition to livestreaming through word clouds created by an analysis of broadcast coverage transcripts. Combined, the evidence directs us to one conclusion—unlike its impact on online print news coverage, the Court's change to livestreaming did not substantially affect the frequency or nature of broadcast coverage of the Court's oral arguments.

VOLUME OF BROADCAST NEWS COVERAGE

Recall from chapter 1 that we analyze eight broadcast networks in our dataset: NBC News, CBS News, ABC News, Fox News, PBS, MSNBC, CNN, and Fox Business Network.[3] While chapter 2 explores online print media coverage of these outlets, we also are interested in the broadcast coverage of each network, as print and broadcast coverage differ significantly in how they report the news.[4] To this end, we collected broadcast transcripts about what transpired at the Court's oral arguments from these news networks across our oral argument sessions of interest (the October 2019, 2020, and 2021 Terms). With these data in hand, which include 282 stories about the Court's arguments, we first examine the volume of such broadcast coverage to determine whether the number of stories produced changed with the Court's transition to livestreaming. The results are different than what we found for online print media.

Figure 4.1 depicts the number of broadcast stories across our sessions of interest, with the black bar indicating the May 2020 session, the initial session of livestreaming. Before the Court began livestreaming, the average number of stories produced across an oral argument session was 18.8. Once May 2020 hit, we see that there was *not* a spike in coverage. For that initial

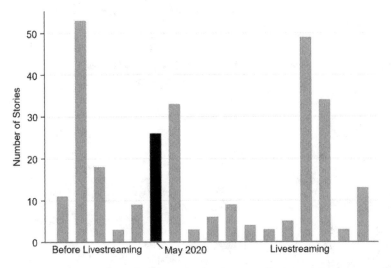

Figure 4.1   Number of Broadcast News Stories about Orally Argued Cases (2019–2021 Terms).

month of livestreaming, there were twenty-six broadcast stories. However, there are other sessions before livestreaming, like November 2019, and after livestreaming, such as sessions across October and November 2021, that received more coverage than the May 2020 session. On average, excluding May 2020, there were 14.7 stories produced per session after livestreaming began. When we include May 2020, this bumps to 15.7, which still indicates less broadcast coverage, although slight, after the Court's transition to livestreaming compared to pre-livestreaming coverage. In other words, unlike the short-term bump in coverage from online print media sources, broadcast coverage did not increase in the short term nor in the long term.

Even though figure 4.1 does not comport with our main hypotheses, interesting variation in the data still exists. Thus, we next examine the extent to which individual broadcast outlets responded differently to increased access. Specifically, table 4.1 comports with figure 4.1 as it indicates that the May 2020 session received coverage but that four sessions before or after it received even more coverage. None of the outlets in our dataset spent considerably more time covering the Court's arguments during the May 2020 session, either. CNN produced the most stories that session, covering cases such as *Trump v. Vance* (2020), *Chiafalo v. Washington* (2020), *United States Patent and Trademark Office v. Booking.com* (2020), and *Little Sisters of the Poor v. Pennsylvania* (2020). MSNBC comes next at six stories with Fox following at five stories.

Chapter 4

Table 4.1 Number of Broadcast News Stories about Supreme Court Orally Argued Cases (2019–2021 Terms)

OA Session	NBC	CBS	ABC	Fox	PBS	MSNBC	CNN	Total by Session
Oct. 2019	0	1	0	0	2	0	8	11
Nov. 2019	1	5	3	3	6	5	30	53
Dec. 2019	0	3	1	0	4	3	7	18
Jan. 2020	0	0	0	2	1	0	0	3
Feb. 2020	0	1	0	0	1	0	7	9
May 2020	*1*	*2*	*0*	*5*	*3*	*6*	*9*	*26*
Oct. 2020	1	0	1	1	3	4	23	33
Nov. 2020	0	0	0	0	1	1	1	3
Dec. 2020	0	1	0	2	0	2	1	6
Jan. 2021	0	0	0	0	0	0	0	0
Feb. 2021	0	0	0	2	0	3	4	9
Mar. 2021	0	2	0	1	1	0	0	4
Apr. 2021	0	1	0	0	1	0	1	3
Oct. 2021	0	0	1	1	2	0	1	5
Nov. 2021	1	4	5	2	2	14	21	49
Dec. 2021	3	4	1	2	1	7	16	34
Jan. 2022	0	0	0	0	0	0	0	0
Feb. 2022	0	0	0	0	0	0	0	0
Mar. 2022	1	0	0	1	1	0	0	3
Apr. 2022	2	4	0	3	0	1	3	13
Total by Outlet	10	28	12	25	29	46	132	282

The data in figure 4.1 and table 4.1 do not include stories that ran about the actual transition to livestreaming itself. Recall that we are only interested in coverage of the 174 cases in our dataset. Of the broadcast outlets in our sample, Fox News, PBS News, and CNN are the only three outlets to report on the Court's transition to livestreaming on its first day, May 4, 2020, by covering arguments in *Patent and Trademark Office v. Booking.com* (2020). Fox News framed the transition as "a day of firsts at the US Supreme Court . . . The first time audio of the Court's arguments was heard live by the world, and the first arguments by telephone. All it took was a global pandemic." Similarly, PBS said it was an argument "unlike any other it had held before, not for the legal issues at stake, but for the logistics of holding proceedings during a pandemic over the telephone and broadcasting live as it happened." Finally, CNN called it an "extraordinary first today." All three outlets told the public how the move to livestreaming represented a change to the Court's internal rules. They explained how livestreaming was "a first for the Supreme Court" and, instead of "a very hot bench," the justices spoke "one by one." They also talked about the "few glitches" that occurred but "all in all, the [C]ourt had to be pretty happy with how the arguments played out today."

It does not appear there was an agreed-upon session with the most newsworthy cases for our outlets of interest. For instance, Fox News produced the most stories across all sessions during May 2020, but MSNBC produced its peak number of stories during the November 2021 session when the Court heard arguments in cases such as *New York State Rifle & Pistol Assn., Inc. v. Bruen* (2022) and *United States v. Texas* (2022). Coverage from PBS and CBS was highest during the November 2019 session," including a discussion of *Department of Homeland Security v. Regents of Univ. of CA* (2020). NBC produced its largest number of stories in December of 2021 by covering *Dobbs v. Jackson Women's Health* (2022). Collectively, this suggests that, perhaps, case salience played a key role in whether these outlets covered a case—which comports somewhat with our findings in chapters 2 and 3—though it is interesting that the volume of coverage varies so much by outlet.

Beyond session-specific data, CNN produced the most stories (132) about the Court's oral arguments, across all our sessions of interest, and the frequency of its coverage did not increase when the Court began livestreaming. In fact, CNN produced the most stories of any session in November 2019. In contrast, NBC produced the fewest stories, with only ten across the three terms in our sample. Compared to coverage from its sister station MSNBC, the discrepancy between coverage is somewhat intuitive because NBC is a broadcast channel that plays primetime shows, daytime shows, children's programming, talk shows, and news shows while MSNBC is exclusively a news channel that provides news coverage twenty-four hours a day, 7 days a week. Combined, none of the individual outlets in our dataset had a boost in coverage during the May 2020 session and beyond when the Court began livestreaming.

The results in figure 4.1 and table 4.1 provide us with clear evidence as to why it is important for us to separate our online print dataset from broadcast. With immediate access to the Court's oral arguments, broadcast media outlets—at least in the aggregate—did not dedicate more airtime to Supreme Court arguments. Perhaps this is because broadcast outlets rely on audio *and* visual images to tell a story and the increased accessibility to audio did not provide broadcast outlets with enough of a multi-sensory appeal: ongoing dialogue, action, and background sounds coupled with visuals. Many broadcast news outlets emphasize stories that contain visuals (Block 1997). For those media outlets in our dataset, it may not have been enough that the Court began to livestream its arguments. Broadcast outlets seek out stories with words, pictures, and sound. If the Court ever decides to bring cameras into the courtroom, it would be interesting to explore whether the frequency of broadcast coverage would change in the same way as did online print media outlets when oral argument audio was livestreamed.

In terms of frequency we consider, finally, coverage by the ideological leaning of the outlet.[5] Here, figure 4.2 shows a pattern similar to the aggregate and individual outlets across left, center, and right-leaning outlets.[6] We categorize outlets in this way because there may be an incentive, for instance, for right-leaning broadcast outlets to cover different cases than left-leaning or center outlets. The average number of stories produced across all sessions is 11.1 for liberal outlets, 1.5 for conservative outlets, and 4.1 for center outlets.[7] Liberal outlets—CNN, MSNBC, and NBC—produced an average of 12.2 stories before livestreaming, 16 stories during the May 2020 session, and 10.1 stories across the remaining sessions for a total of 188 stories.

For the liberal outlets, at least, coverage spiked several times, including before and after livestreaming was introduced. Liberal broadcast outlets produced thirty-six stories in November of 2019, before livestreaming began, when the Court was hearing arguments in *Department of Homeland Security v. Regents of Univ. of CA* (2020). This case was particularly salient, as it was about the Department of Homeland Security's decision to rescind the Deferred Action for Childhood Arrivals program. Coverage also temporarily increased in May 2020 and the following October 2020 session (28 stories). Thus, the evidence is again mixed for our first hypothesis of interest—that the move to livestreaming in May 2020 would drive increased coverage.

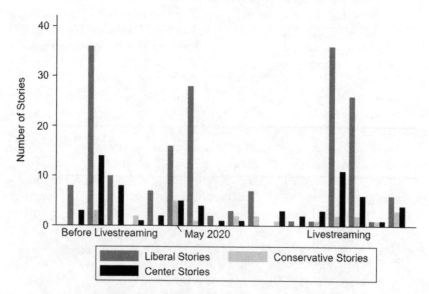

Figure 4.2   Number of Broadcast News Stories about Orally Argued Cases by Ideological Leanings of News Outlets. *Source*: Data based on the Interactive Media Bias Charts: https://adfontesmedia.com/interactive-media-bias-chart/

For conservative coverage, or Fox since it is the only conservative broadcast outlet in the dataset, of the twenty-five stories produced, five were produced during the May 2020 session—the most stories produced in a single session across all twenty sessions. As expected, this uptick in stories does not persist very long. On average, before livestreaming, Fox News produced roughly one story a session about arguments. This increases to five during May 2020 and then to 1.3 stories for all cases after that session. In other words, this provides some support for our *volume hypothesis* because Fox produced more stories in May 2020 and then, like online print media, dropped back to levels seen prior to livestreaming.

The transition to livestreaming also does not seem to have affected coverage in terms of frequency for our more center outlets: PBS, ABC, and CBS. Of the sixty-nine stories produced by these outlets, five were produced when the Court began livestreaming in May 2020, but fourteen were produced during the November 2019 session (before livestreaming), and eleven were produced during the October 2021 session (after livestreaming). On average, these outlets produced 5.6 stories before the May 2020 session, five stories during the May session, and then 3.2 stories on average per session after the initial month of livestreaming.

From the analysis in this section, we conclude that immediate access to the Court's oral argument audio did not alter the *volume* of broadcast coverage in the same clear way it altered coverage by online print news outlets.[8] Certainly, a spike occurred during the May 2020 session for Fox News, and there was an increase in average coverage across liberal outlets in May 2020 and a corresponding decline after that month but, overall, livestreaming did not strongly affect broadcast coverage of the Court's arguments during the May 2020 session and beyond.

NATURE OF BROADCAST NEWS COVERAGE

While livestreaming did not fundamentally affect the number of stories broadcast outlets produced about oral argument, it may have influenced the nature of such coverage. Compared to online print coverage, did broadcast news outlets cover the same cases? What kind of information did these broadcast stories convey? Here we explore the content of these news stories across our three terms of interest.

Before turning to the data, however, we note that broadcast and online print media coverage differs in fundamental ways that influence how we assess and discuss broadcast stories. For broadcast stories, messages are fleeting, especially when compared to online print media coverage. After a television segment runs for fifteen, thirty, or sixty seconds, the message is out of sight and out of sound (Block 1997). This means that broadcast media stories must be quick-hitting whereas print news stories can be longer and much more in-depth. In broadcast journalism, the focus is also on the tonality used by the anchors and their diction (Musburger 2012) as they use the technique of "dramatic unity" to create suspense and reach the climax of a story. Finally, broadcast headlines are usually simple one-liners that provide the audience with cues meant to pique audience interest (Musburger 2012). For example, CBS began its coverage of *Kennedy v. Bremerton School District* (2022) with, "All right, at the Supreme Court, oral arguments began today in one of the most important school prayer cases in more than a decade." This one sentence allowed the audience to quickly know the significance of the case with phrases such as "most important" and "more than a decade."[9]

Before turning to the broadcast news data, consider how this type of coverage differs from online print coverage. Specifically, we examine how one outlet—Fox News—covered the same case across platforms. On March 31, 2021, the justices heard arguments in *NCAA v. Alston* (2021), a consolidated case challenging whether the collegiate sports association's limits on providing compensation and benefits to student-athletes violated federal antitrust law. Consider, first, how Fox's broadcast channel covered the proceedings. Our data show that it was discussed on Bret Baier's show, "Special Report," an evening news and commentary show that has run on the network since 2009. Despite its importance, Baier did not dedicate his entire show, or even a full segment, to this highly consequential case. Rather, it took up just a small part of the show. In fact, it was not until more than midway through it that Bret Baier transitioned to discussing the case:

BAIER: The US Supreme Court heard oral arguments today over how colleges can reward athletes who play at the top levels of football and basketball. The NCAA says if the former college students who brought the case win, it could erase the distinction between professional and college sports.

The athletes say the current rules deprive students of the ability to be rewarded for their athletic talents. So far, the former players have actually won every round of this case. Lower courts have agreed that the NCAA's rules capping education related benefits can violate federal antitrust law.

There is new controversy tonight over the World Health Organization report on where the coronavirus came from, its origins. The head of that organization is openly complaining about the lack of data from Chinese officials. Senior foreign affairs correspondent Greg Palkot has the latest tonight from London.

To put this in context, before ever even discussing the case, the panelists on the show focused on an infrastructure plan in Pittsburgh, coronavirus vaccines, ballots, plant closures, and a whole host of other topics. It did so with a host of appearances too—Peter Doocy, Jonathan Serrie, Casey

Stegall, Matt Finn, Chad Pergram, Mark Meredith, and Greg Palkot. While the coverage itself ballooned to over 7,000 words, only a handful of sentences were dedicated to the Court's arguments—the general account above and then when Morgan Ortagus turned back to the case in her wrap up:

> ORTAGUS: . . . The Supreme Court could transform college athletics with a ruling that says pay college athletes. I think it's about time. I wish Michigan would have won last night, but the fact that they played at 10:00 last night and they are college athletes, this isn't amateurism anymore. They should be paid.

The coverage on Fox's "Special Report" contrasts with Fox's online print coverage about this case, which totaled almost 1,000 words. Unlike the broadcast story, the online print news story gave consumers deeper background information and an extensive overview of the case, direct oral argument quotes from Justices Elena Kagan, Brett Kavanaugh, Sonia Sotomayor, and Chief Justice John Roberts and offered insights from athletic programs across the country. Below we display the first 200 words of the story to provide context.[10]

> It's the legal and financial version of "March Madness."
>
> With sports fans focused on the college women's and men's basketball tournament, the US Supreme Court served as referee Wednesday in a high-stakes competition over the future of amateur athletics.
>
> The justices heard 95 minutes of oral arguments over whether the NCAA—intercollegiate sports' main governing body—is using its anti-trust protections to illegally cap non-cash "education-based benefits" for student-athletes.
>
> It is the first time the high court is considering the NCAA's business model in nearly four decades. The very future of college sports—and the big money for many schools that come with it—could be at stake.
>
> The case comes amid growing calls for greater student compensation, especially in those profitable sports like Division I basketball and football. Current rules do not allow students to be paid to play, and scholarship money and other benefits are strictly capped. But a high court ruling for the players could allow schools to offer additional, wide-ranging "education-related" benefits—like post-graduate scholarships, paid internships and computers. A majority of the court appeared ready to side, at least in part, with the players, several offering skepticism at the NCAA's position.

To reiterate, because the differences are so stark between broadcast coverage and print coverage, we examine the nature of broadcast coverage differently from online print coverage in chapter 3. We first assess the most common cases that broadcast outlets covered. Then we describe coverage using word clouds, or images composed of words used in the broadcast transcripts, in which the size of each word indicates its frequency.

Consider first the cases covered across our argument sessions of interest. Table 4.2 shows the top ten cases covered in broadcast stories about the Court's oral arguments. *Department of Homeland Security v. Regents of Univ. of CA* (2020), a case about the Department of Homeland Security's decision to rescind the Deferred Action for Childhood Arrivals (DACA) program received the most coverage—accounting for forty-nine stories in the sample. Media outlets framed this argument as having high stakes for the public at large. For instance, ABC referred to it as a "dreamers showdown" as thousands demonstrated outside of the Court building during the hearing. Similarly, CNN called the arguments "consequential," and Fox framed them as the Court determining the "legal fate of illegal immigrants who came to the country as children."[11] Additionally, the broadcast media's deep dive into the DACA case—which occurred prior to livestreaming—suggests the nature of broadcast coverage is driven by something other than immediate access to the Court's proceedings.

One key possibility is that broadcast coverage of arguments is driven by the salience of the issue surrounding a case.[12] This is evidenced by the second and third most covered cases in table 4.2. Indeed, *Dobbs v. Jackson Women's Health Org.* (2022) and *California v. Texas* (2020) dealt with highly salient issues—abortion and the Affordable Care Act, respectively. As to the former, outlets were quick with catchy headlines to grab people's attention. NBC labeled the Court's arguments as "dramatic" and said the justices were considering "the most significant challenge to abortion rights in at least three decades . . . [it] is a direct challenge to the landmark ruling of *Roe v. Wade*." CNN set a similar tone with its coverage: "the Supreme

Table 4.2   Top Ten Most Covered Orally Argued Cases by Broadcast Media (2019–2021 Terms)

Case Name	Session	Stories	Pre-Argument Stories
DHS v. Regents of Univ. of CA (Consolidated)	Nov. 2019	49	8
Dobbs v. Jackson Women's Health Org.	Dec. 2021	34	28
California v. Texas	Nov. 2020	34	11
United States v. Texas	Nov. 2021	33	2
Trump v. Mazars/Trump v. Vance	**May 2020**	**19**	**23**
New York State Rifle and Pistol Assn. v. Bruen	Nov. 2021	16	0
Brnovich v. DNC, AZ Republican Party v. DNC	Mar. 2021	9	0
R.G. and G.R. Harris Funeral Homes, Inc. v. EEOC	Oct. 2019	9	14
New York State Rifle and Pistol Assn., Inc. v. City of NY	Dec. 2019	8	4
Biden v. Texas	Apr. 2022	7	3

Court heard arguments in the case that could roll back the right Americans have had for nearly 50 years." Interestingly, Fox focused on the commentary surrounding the arguments, perhaps in direct response to how more liberal outlets such as NBC and CNN perceived the arguments. It introduced its story with the following: "Well, a major abortion case went before the Supreme Court today. There has been a lot of commentary on it, most of it has been absurd."

Coverage of *California v. Texas* (2020), a case about the constitutionality of the 2010 Affordable Care Act, focused on the series of events happening at the Court and in the broader political context of the day. The Court heard arguments in this case about Obamacare "just a week after the election," as CNN put it. This portended coverage throughout the November 2020 argument sessions. For instance, MSNBC covered *Trump v. New York* (2020) and said,

> it turns out those calls on election night that so angered the Trump campaign, here we are with Biden certified as the winner there. But let's go now to the Supreme Court where oral arguments have wrapped up in a major case that could have sweeping implications for how you're represented in Congress.

To this end, we note that, oftentimes, when broadcast outlets discuss the Court's arguments, they incorporate commentary about the potential policy consequences of a decision and often use the word "you" to make it clear that it is the public who is affected by such decisions. This essentially turns the Court's arguments into human interest stories, connecting arguments to people and their problems or concerns. In contrast, print media outlets tend to exclusively focus on the cases themselves—what was said and who said what. Perhaps this is because, as we discussed above, broadcast outlets require visuals as they relate stories and, because the Court does not allow cameras to cover argument sessions, this is an alternative way for broadcast outlets to cover proceedings in a way that is engaging to their audiences. Take, for example, CNN's story about *California v. Texas* (2020):

> CNN SEN. CHRIS COONS (D-DE): Let me, if I could, put up another poster that may make this a little sharper in a way, that is, the political branch is not the judicial branch.
>
> The Supreme Court's going to hear arguments—as I've said—in this case a week after the election.
>
> [15:00:02]
>
> And most Americans are probably surprised to even hear about it. When I talked to a constituent, Carrie (ph), who has a pre-existing condition, she

was surprised this was even in front of the court. She said, "I thought this was settled."

Carrie (ph) owns a small business, she has a daughter she's raising. And before the ACA, she had to spend $800 a month for insurance that she described as "junk," left her afraid of even going to the doctor's office or needing drugs. And because of the ACA, she's been able to get better quality insurance that she can afford and she's got both type 2 diabetes and high blood pressure.

But the ACA guarantees she can't be denied insurance or made to pay higher premiums either because of her gender or because of these pre- existing conditions. She expressed to me astonishment.

Many of us are engaged and interested in this because we care about the Constitution, we care about constitutional law and the ways in which it impacts a majority of all Americans—frankly, all Americans. Help me explain to her how is it that the Affordable Care Act, settled eight years ago, is back in front of the Supreme Court?[13]

The story connects the arguments to a constituent, Carrie, who will be affected in a consequential way based on how the justices ultimately decide. Specifically, she had been able to pay low prices for her medications and doc-tor visits and believed the Court's involvement with the ACA "was settled." CNN also framed the Court's decision-making process with appeals to the Constitution: "Many of us are engaged and interested in this because we care about the Constitution, we care about constitutional law and the ways in which it impacts a majority of all Americans." Here, the network seemed to be saying that people are concerned with what the Constitution says about the Affordable Care Act—a legalistic approach to interpreting case law.

Beyond the top three cases from table 4.2, broadcast outlets also covered cases such as *United States v. Texas* (2021), *Trump v. Mazars/Trump v. Vance* (2020), and *New York State Rifle and Pistol Assn. v. Bruen* (2022). Most intriguing is that *Trump v. Mazars* and *Trump v. Vance* are the only cases on this list that emanated from the initial livestreaming session in May 2020. These cases involved subpoenas issued by committees of the US House of Representatives to obtain the tax returns of former President Donald Trump. This finding suggests that broadcast media outlets did not pay as much atten-tion to the Court's decision to livestream its arguments as did online print media outlets and did not alter how they covered the Court as a result. Instead, the coverage seems to be driven more by the salience of a case.

This contrasts with online print coverage of arguments (see chapter 2), where the top four covered arguments came from May 2020: *Patent & Trademark v. Booking.com* (2020), *Trump v. Mazars/ Trump v. Vance* (2020), *Chiafalo v. Washington* (2020), and *Little Sisters of the Poor v. Pennsylvania* (2020). Again, compared to online print news it seems that broadcast outlets paid even less attention to the Court's decision to livestream—only PBS, CNN, and Fox produced broadcast stories about *Booking.com* while every single online print outlet produced at least one story about arguments in the case! The key takeaway is that broadcast news media coverage did not change in the short term or the long term after livestreaming permitted immediate access to oral arguments. This adds additional evidence to our argument about why we separately examine these different types of coverage.

Moving away from aggregate case-level data, we now continue our investigation of the nature of broadcast coverage by examining commentary contained in this coverage.[14] We begin with mentions of the justices and questions they asked during the arguments. While, from time to time, there was commentary about what the justices said, two justices were singled out in the transcripts—Coney Barrett and Thomas. Barrett began to hear arguments at the start of the Court's November 2020 session, and broadcast outlets provided commentary about her involvement in questioning the attorneys (Houston et al. 2022). For instance, MSNBC offered this back-and-forth between Brian Williams and for Neal Katyal (former Principal Deputy Solicitor General of the United States):

> *BRIAN WILLIAMS*: Neal Katyal, there's a lot of anxiety on the left about the so called New Look Supreme Court just because I'm curious, I assumed today your virtual argument before the court included Justice Barrett, and I'm curious, was she an active participant in questioning?
> *NEAL KATYAL*: Yeah, she was an active participant, asked great questions, balanced questions at both sides. She's hit the ground running. And so, you know, as my first argument in 42 without Justice Ginsburg, and, you know, in some ways, I was glad it was telephonic because otherwise, I think I would have shed some tears. But I thought Justice Barrett handled the, you know, our first week of arguments really, really well.

When the May 2020 session began, broadcast outlets were also enamored of Thomas' participation given that he was largely silent during oral arguments for most of his tenure on the bench.[15] On CNN, Legal Analyst Elie Honig and former Chief Legal Analyst Jeffrey Toobin discussed Thomas' contributions at argument during the May 2020 session. As Toobin put it:

> As someone who has followed the Supreme Court for a long time, it's a very weird experience to hear the court this way. Just one oddity of all this is I think many people know that Clarence Thomas in the courtroom, you know, goes years without answering questions. In the telephone arguments, where the

justices go one at a time, the Chief Justice calls on them one at a time, Clarence Thomas is asking lots of questions. I don't know such a big distinction between telephone arguments and real-life arguments but it's just a big difference. Does that matter in the outcome? I sort of doubt it. But it's still just interesting given how the court has evolved.

Fox News went a step further, as it played audio of Thomas speaking during the argument in *Booking.com*!

SPUNT: Today, a rare moment by Justice Clarence Thomas who once went a decade without asking a single question during an oral argument.
J.G. ROBERTS: Justice Thomas?
CLARENCE THOMAS, ASSOCIATE JUSTICE, SUPREME COURT OF THE UNITED STATES: Yes, could booking acquire an 800 number, for example, that's a vanity number 1-800 Booking, for example?

While broadcast outlets focused on Barrett and Thomas, they also used the proceedings to offer predictions about how the justices would ultimately decide the case.[16] Several examples make this point. First, immediately after arguments in *Trump v. New York* (2020), commentators at MSNBC tried to predict what the Court was going to do with the US Census. As Pete Williams put it:

My guess is that they will not block the administration in this initial decision from doing this. They'll wait to see what happens. They'll wait to see how many figures the Census Bureau actually gives the president, whether that would make a difference in reapportionment, and maybe then entertain new lawsuits to try to block that.

Further, in CNN's coverage of *Trump v. Vance* (2020), Legal Analyst Elie Honig discussed each justice as she tried to figure out how the Court would vote on the constitutionality of the subpoena issued against Trump:

ELIE HONIG: Yes, so, what I noticed is that the four traditionally liberal Justices, Ginsburg, Sotomayor, Breyer, and Kagan were really dug in. They were really committed. They did not seem to be giving any ground whatsoever. They seemed set on holding up these subpoenas. The four conservative, traditionally conservative Justices did seem to be a little bit uneasy with some of the positions that were being taken. And I think Chief Justice Roberts is desperately trying to find middle ground. I do think both of these cases ultimately are going to come out against the President. I think especially the case involving the Manhattan D.A. I think we could see an 8-1, 9-0 ruling upholding that subpoena against Donald Trump.

CONTENT OF NEWS STORIES
THROUGH WORD CLOUDS

Our final analysis of content coverage from a broadcast perspective focuses on word clouds. These clouds represent the frequency of words used by media outlets in their stories about arguments.[17] We compiled all transcripts from our sample of broadcast stories into a spreadsheet and separated them by whether they pertained to cases heard before livestreaming, during the first month of livestreaming, or after the first month of livestreaming. We next limited the transcripts to include only the text about oral argument. We then produced word clouds to depict words used by media outlets in this more focused coverage. The bigger a word appears the more often it is mentioned within the transcripts of a given time period.

First, we examine the word cloud in figure 4.3 that depicts transcripts before the May 2020 transition to livestreaming (October 2019 through March 2020). From this cloud, words such as "supreme" and "court" are the most commonly used ones but once we set these words aside, the next most common words include "administration," "dreamers," "immigrants," and "DACA." These words reflect arguments heard in *Department of Homeland Security v. Regents of Univ. of CA* (2020), which was argued in November 2019. Recall that, of the ninety-four stories produced before livestreaming, forty-nine of them were about this case.

When we examine a word cloud from the ten cases argued during the first month of livestreaming (May 2020), figure 4.4 demonstrates that words including "president," "subpoena," Trump," and "financial" are the most frequently used. During this session, much of the coverage focused on *Trump*

Figure 4.3   Word Cloud of Top Fifty Words Used in Broadcast News Transcripts about Orally Argued Cases before Livestreaming Began (2019 Term). *Source:* Created with https://www.freewordcloudgenerator.com

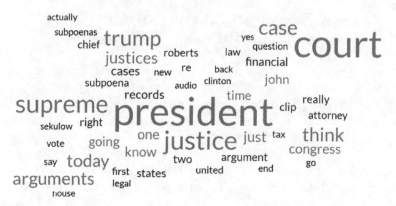

Figure 4.4 Word Cloud of Top Fifty Words Used in Broadcast News Transcripts about Orally Argued Cases during First Month of Livestreaming (2019 Term). *Source:* Created with https://www.freewordcloudgenerator.com

v. Mazars/*Trump v. Vance* (2020), a case where President Trump asked the Supreme Court to block a New York grand jury subpoena requesting that he turn over his financial records. Of the twenty-six broadcast stories produced during this session, nineteen of them were about these arguments.

Interestingly, while the words "audio" and "clip" are frequently used, they are not as common as the words used to describe the Trump cases. Indeed, once we examined the thirty-one mentions of "audio," only fifteen were about the Court's audio; the other sixteen were when the broadcast transcripts inserted audio clips into their stories with the commands "(BEGIN AUDIO CLIP)" and "(END AUDIO CLIP)." Of the forty-four times "clip" was used, only two of them referred to an audio clip; the other forty-two times captured instances where clip was used to show either video or audio. The only time the words "livestream" or "livestreaming" were used happened during coverage of arguments in *United States Patent and Trademark Office v. Booking.com* (2020) when Yamiche Alcindor (PBS News) said, "But now that the court has adjusted to the times, at least for these first two weeks in May, will audio livestreaming stick around, even after the pandemic has passed?"

While "telephone" is not listed as a most common word, it is used fourteen times with twelve of those instances where broadcast outlets discussed the Court's telephonic arguments. These stories framed arguments as "being heard by telephone because of the pandemic with the public listening in, in real time" and discussing another day "of historic arguments, all via telephone" (CNN and MSNBC, respectively). During this May 2020 session, then, broadcast stories did not really touch on the Court's transition to livestreaming. Rather, the transcripts indicate broadcast outlets continued normal coverage—discussing salient cases as they routinely do (Slotnick and Segal 1998). This adds

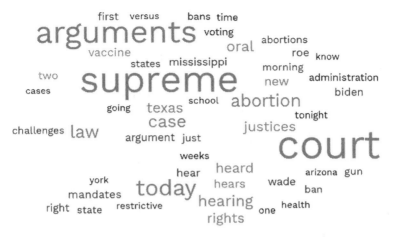

Figure 4.5   Word Cloud of Top Fifty Words Used in Broadcast News Transcripts about Orally Argued Cases during the 2020 and 2021 Terms. *Source*: Created with https://www.freewordcloudgenerator.com

additional support to our general finding that the transition to livestreaming did not substantially affect broadcast coverage of the Court's oral arguments.

Finally, figure 4.5 focuses on coverage of all livestreamed cases after the initial May 2020 session. Here, words such as "Texas," "Mississippi," "roe," "wade," "abortions," and "health" are the most frequent as broadcast outlets spent a great deal of time discussing *United States v. Texas* (2021) and *Dobbs v. Jackson Women's Health Org.* (2022), both cases about whether the Constitution confers a right to abortion. "York" and "gun," on the other hand, are about *New York State Rifle and Pistol Assn. v. Bruen*. Unlike the transcripts from the May 2020 session, words such as "audio," "clip," and "telephone" are not commonly discussed.

All in all, these word clouds reflect the findings in table 4.2 about the top cases with the most stories; there is nothing noteworthy that distinguishes the coverage of livestreamed sessions from the non-livestreamed sessions. This contributes to our argument that livestreaming did not change the nature of broadcast coverage. While the actual topic of livestreaming was discussed in the short term, broad coverage during the May 2020 session and all other periods of interest focused on the most salient cases.

CONCLUSION

Combined with the results reported in chapters 2 and 3, the data show that, while online print media outlets changed coverage of Supreme Court oral arguments in the short term when livestreaming was introduced, broadcast outlets generally did not. However, our findings indicate that for both types of outlets, coverage of livestreamed cases looks similar to that of pre-livestreamed cases in the long term. Given that the public relies on news media coverage to learn about the Court and its decisions, the next chapter discusses the implications of our findings for the public's understanding of and perspective on the Court and for proposals to further increase access to the Court, such as video coverage.

Conclusion

The historic session began at the usual time of 10am ET, when Marshal Pamela Talkin called the court to order and Chief Justice John Roberts announced the day's case . . . The experiment could propel the court to routinely livestream its arguments. Or it could just be an extraordinary exception to the court's sustained opposition to broadening the audience that can hear, if not see, its work live.[1]

For the first time in its 230-year history, the high court offered a live audio stream of an oral argument, going far beyond its usual protocol and giving advocates of greater transparency hope it will become a trend.[2]

This May 4, 2020, coverage by *The Guardian* and *USA Today* is indicative of just how clearly the media understood the historic nature of allowing everyone, worldwide, to listen live to the US Supreme Court's oral arguments. It also piqued our interest and led us to ponder the extent to which the media reacted to this instantaneous access with changes in how they covered these proceedings. And the media did react, at least initially. This leads to the much broader question we consider in here: *does it matter how news media outlets portray the nation's highest court?*

We argue how media cover of the Court is absolutely important because news outlets serve as the critical intermediary between it and the public. Indeed, the public relies on the media for information about the Court and the justices have (at least historically) understood this reliance (Leighley 2004; Davis 1994; Davis and Strickler 2000) and, by extension, the role media coverage plays in shaping public support for the Court. The key to this connection is that support from the public is vital to maintaining the Court's institutional standing, which is its main source of power. In other words, in the absence of electoral accountability, the justices derive institutional support through public belief in the legitimacy of the decisions they make. Thus, if the Court lacks public support, it risks less than full compliance with its decisions or, in the extreme, having them ignored altogether (see, e.g., Black et al. 2023; Wedeking and Zilis 2022).

The problem is that public support is tied, at least in part, to the public's understanding of what the Court does. However, the technical legal language justices and lawyers use to discuss the oral arguments in cases the Court hears, combined with limited access to the courtroom itself, make it impractical for most individuals to learn directly from these proceedings and the decisions the justices make. This is where news coverage comes into play. News media outlets employ their discretion to create, write, air, or stream stories about the Court using less technical, more general, language that helps the public develop views about the Court, its decision-making process, and the decisions the justices make (e.g., Wedeking and Zilis 2022; Zilis 2015; Linos and Twist 2016; Hitt and Searles 2018; Slotnick and Segal 1998). Combined, such information ultimately helps the public assess the Court's institutional legitimacy (e.g., Caldeira and Gibson 1992; Gibson and Caldeira 2009; Johnston and Bartels 2010).

The advent of livestreamed oral argument audio in May 2020 had the potential to alter media coverage of oral arguments and, by extension, public perceptions of the justices and the nation's court of last resort. To examine this possibility, we investigated the *volume* and *nature of coverage* surrounding these proceedings for the highest circulating online print and broadcast media outlets in the United States. We expected that, in the short term, news media outlets would respond to the novelty and reduced barriers to timely reporting provided by livestreamed oral argument with increased and more in-depth coverage. However, we also anticipated that coverage in the long term would revert back to the norms of pre-livestreamed reporting as the novelty of immediate access wore off and as competing opportunities for coverage beyond the Court emerged. Our findings generally support both of these expectations.

SUMMARY OF OUR FINDINGS

With respect to the volume of coverage, we consistently find that the initial period of livestreaming (May 2020) dramatically increased the number of stories in online print outlets but that this was a short-term disruption to the status quo. Indeed, the historic nature, and novelty, of the Court's decision to livestream propelled four cases heard during May 2020—*Patent & Trademark v. Booking.com* (2020), *Trump v Mazars* (2020), *Chiafalo v. Washington* (2020), and *Little Sisters of the Poor v. Pennsylvania* (2020)—to be the most covered in our three-term sample. These cases were put in this position despite ranking lower than many other cases on traditional measures of case salience. Importantly, this pattern of a temporary spike in the number of online print stories holds for news media outlets across the ideological spectrum.

With respect to the nature of online print coverage, we find a similar pattern with the depth of coverage increasing temporarily. First, the length of stories and the use of direct quotations from oral arguments—both at the aggregate and individual justice level (with the key exception of Justice Clarence Thomas)—increased substantially with the advent of livestreaming. However, while livestreaming mitigated significant barriers to additional in-depth reporting, story length and the use of quotes by online print news media ultimately looked, in the long term, very much like the coverage before livestreaming began. Embedding audio clips within stories is one rare example of a long-term change in coverage since the advent of livestreaming, but importantly, this new phenomenon occurs in only a small proportion of stories.

Second, coverage containing the most quotations also disproportionately favored cases heard during the first month of livestreaming, which also indicates that the depth of coverage increased in the short but not in the long term. Third, we find that, while there is some variation at the individual level, as a group, justices' questions and comments during livestreamed oral arguments were not taken out of context in online print media coverage to any greater degree than they were prior to livestreaming. Finally, the data demonstrate smaller outlets that did not typically cover oral arguments (e.g., *Boston Globe*, *New York Post*, *Newsday*, etc.) temporarily made room for such stories when livestreaming began and the novelty of this development was at its peak. But they did not cover these cases with their own reporters. Rather, they managed the costs of such coverage by reprinting articles from the *Associated Press*, or from other major newspapers, rather than by generating original stories.

Our findings on how online print media altered coverage of oral arguments throughout our sample of cases are also clear. Less clear is how broadcast media outlets reacted, if at all, to the advent of livestreaming. In fact, the broadcast channels in the sample showed that they neither increased coverage nor changed the nature of their coverage. While this cuts against our theoretical argument and empirical findings about online print media coverage in the short term, the findings are consistent with the way in which broadcast media differs from print media. Indeed, chapter 1 lays out the argument that broadcast messages must be immediately understood so their stories need to be shorter than do print or online versions of print stories.

Thus, we are not altogether surprised that these findings did not comport fully with the online print media findings in chapters 2 and 3. Importantly though, for both online print and broadcast outlets, our analysis shows that livestreamed oral argument audio did not lead to significant long-term changes in coverage. In the end, the combination of findings from these chapters has major implications for our understanding of the relationship between the Court, the media, and the public.

IMPLICATIONS OF OUR FINDINGS

Livestreaming oral argument is part of a long list of ways in which access to the US Supreme Court has gradually increased over time, including the advent of publicly accessible transcripts and audio recordings available after the proceedings. The fundamental argument for greater access to the Court is that the ability to observe, know, and understand how government institutions function is a critical feature of a democratic society. Such transparency promotes trust in, and the legitimacy of, such institutions. With oral argument being the only public portion of the Court's consideration of cases the justices decide, access to these proceedings is a critical component of the Court's transparency and, ultimately, its legitimacy as one of the three coequal branches of the federal government.

Our findings suggest that there is room for the Court to move closer to the democratic ideal of transparency in government without risking its legitimacy. Indeed, the analysis indicates the increased access gained by livestreaming does not come at a significant cost to the Court in the form of long-term changes in media coverage of its decision-making process. If greater access to oral argument proceedings changed the news coverage the public relies on to be informed about the Court, this could portend a risk to the Court's legitimacy (see e.g., Black et al. 2023). Instead, however, our analysis indicates news outlets only temporarily increased or changed their approach to oral argument coverage when immediate access was provided via livestreaming. The pressures of the twenty-four-hour news cycle likely constrain the extent to which media outlets intensify scrutiny of a single institution or entity such as the Court, even when access to that institution increases and barriers to coverage decrease.

Finally, our findings speak to the theoretical and empirical work about how institutions react to major events such as the COVID-19 pandemic. Indeed, the theory of institutional change and adaptation to such change suggests that social, political, and legal actors can and do react when the context of the world changes. However, they also often refine their behavior if the institutional change becomes the new normal, as we saw online print news media outlets do in the long term after the advent of livestreaming. This demonstrates the degree to which our findings are applicable well beyond media coverage of US Supreme Court oral arguments.

Additional proposals for increasing access to the Court and its decision-making abound. Our analysis informs the debate surrounding these proposals, and we conclude the book by discussing two of them.

Permanent Commitment to Livestreaming Oral Argument Audio

As we draft the conclusion of the book, the Court is in the midst of its 2022 October Term, during which time it continues to livestream oral arguments but without committing to permanently doing so. Our analysis did not identify a major negative impact of the transition to livestreamed audio. On the other hand, court watchers, the press, and opinion leaders hailed the increase in transparency, expressing enthusiasm and encouraging the Court to continue this practice. For example, a *Washington Post* Editorial Board opinion piece applauded the move saying, "good for the Court for embracing transparency and engagement with regular Americans."[3] Further, a March 2022 letter from 40 attorneys—who have argued a combined 464 cases before the Supreme Court—to Roberts requested that the livestream be a permanent fixture of oral arguments. Within the letter the attorneys noted the benefits that livestreaming has produced:

> scores of law professors have used the streams as teaching tools of appellate advocacy. Hundreds of media outlets have linked to them so listeners and viewers could hear directly from the justices, unfiltered and in real time, about the issues the Court was grappling with. And tens of thousands of Americans have come to understand the seriousness and the care with which you and your colleagues treat each case and each advocate who comes before the Court.[4]

Since the Court has long been perceived as the most secretive of the federal institutions of government (see, e.g., Black and Johnson 2019), our findings suggest that continuing, indefinitely, to livestream oral arguments could enhance the Court's reputation in the eyes of the public as a transparent institution. At a minimum it would show goodwill toward the public who, based on data we present here, craves such access—especially at the beginning of terms and in salient cases.

Video Coverage of Oral Argument

Beyond oral argument audio, court watchers, elected officials, and the public have repeatedly indicated a desire for additional access to the Court in the form of video coverage. As with audio, video coverage could be livestreamed or recorded and released at the end of argument days or argument weeks. The potential for educational and other benefits associated with increased access, more generally, also applies to video coverage. And this is not an altogether brand-new idea. Many state courts of last resort and three federal circuit courts already allow cameras in their courtrooms—at least some of the time (Kromphardt and Bolton 2022). So, too, do courts of last resort in Australia, Brazil, Canada, and the United Kingdom (Black et al. 2023). As the US Supreme Court continues to hear calls to place cameras in the courtroom, our results further inform the justices about the potential consequences of such a move.

Indeed, while video of oral arguments would increase transparency, the justices have expressed concern that video coverage would negatively impact the Court. For example, Thomas has warned about the potential negative consequences of video cameras in the Court, saying, "It runs the risk of undermining the manner in which we consider the cases. Certainly, it will change our proceedings. And I don't think for the better."[5] Another possibility is that news outlets might focus on short, unrepresentative video clips that would harm the Court's legitimacy. Video coverage might also disproportionately favor conflictual aspects of oral argument, obscuring the norm of collegiality and decorum typically present, or creating opportunities for conflictual behavior or grandstanding to be rewarded by news media attention. This type of coverage could be dangerous for the Court since other work has shown that watching contentious exchanges between attorneys and justices may have a negative impact on the Court's legitimacy (Black et al. 2023).

Importantly, the justices' and advocates' words, verbal inflections, and tone of voice are evident in both audio and visual recordings. The core difference with video as compared to audio coverage is the visual component (Black et al. 2023). Depending on the setup of the equipment (e.g., wide-angle shots versus close-ups and static versus dynamic angles), video coverage might uniquely convey the facial expressions and other body language of individuals involved in oral arguments. Such indicators—along with media outlets' discretion over how video would be included in coverage—have the potential to enhance, complement, or alter the public's understanding of what transpires during Supreme Court oral arguments. Further, since video (with audio) is typically considered even more engaging than audio alone (Black et al. 2023; Kromphardt and Bolton 2022), video coverage might also increase news media and public engagement with the Court.

As a result of this visual difference, our analysis of the Court's use of livestreamed audio cannot fully foretell the consequences of allowing video coverage. However, it offers the best data currently available to inform this debate. In particular, our finding that online print media coverage temporarily changed with the availability of instant access to oral argument audio, but that this change did not persist in the long term, suggests a similar evolution might occur if video coverage is introduced. In other words, our analysis leads us to expect an initial wave of special coverage featuring the novel and historic nature of such a shift in access to the Supreme Court. This may include increased volume of video coverage, increased use of justices' questions and comments (along with attorneys' responses to them), and additional uses of embedded audio/video in online print *and* broadcast stories.

It is this possible increase in volume and change to the nature of coverage that so concerns the justices when they consider placing cameras in their courtroom. But our findings should give them some comfort because if the media react in the same way to cameras as they did to the advent of livestreaming then the justices would not have long to worry. Most specifically, the spike, and then transition to occasional use of embedded audio clips, from oral argument exemplifies this pattern (see figure 3.7 in chapter 3). Oral argument, particularly in salient cases, would likely receive some additional attention, just as it has before and during cases with livestreamed audio but, by and large, the media interest is likely, ultimately, to wane.

FUTURE RESEARCH

While we examine media coverage of Supreme Court oral arguments in a host of ways, future research could further investigate the content of this coverage. For example, it is possible that the language or tone used by reporters has changed along with the advent of livestreaming. Future work could use text and sentiment analysis to better understand how the news media cover the Supreme Court and, by extension, the flow of information to the public. In addition, future research could build on our analysis by assessing individuals' responses to livestreamed oral argument audio or news media coverage containing audio clips. Such work would offer further insight into the potential effects of increased access to Supreme Court oral argument.

CONCLUDING THOUGHTS

Transparency in government institutions has been a rallying cry from the public and the media in recent years. The public health risks of the COVID-19 pandemic forced the US Supreme Court, and government institutions more broadly, to reconsider what access to institutions can and should look like. Increased access to government institutions allows people to engage in and witness historical events. The number of people who listened to live oral argument audio, especially for salient cases, indicates that the public wants to engage directly with the Court and the government.

Our findings demonstrate that the benefits of increased transparency offered by livestreaming oral argument audio have not come with significant disadvantages for the Court in terms of long-term changes in news media coverage of its proceedings. These findings inform consideration of other potential expansions in transparency at the Court and for other government institutions. While a tipping point may exist, the evidence offers encouragement that enhanced transparency can be achieved without sacrificing the Court's legitimacy or the legitimacy of other institutions that make similar changes.

Appendix

Variable Codebook and Additional Tables and Models

VARIABLES CODED FOR EACH NEWS SOURCE (ONLINE PRINT AND BROADCAST)

UniqueCaseID: Each case is assigned its own number.

Number	Case Name
1	Kahler v. Kansas
2	Peter v. Nantkwest, Inc.
3	Ramos v. Louisiana
4	Bostock v. Clayton Cty., GA (Consolidated)
5	R.G. & G.R. Harris Funeral Homes, Inc. v. EEOC
6	Financial Oversight Bd. V. Aurelius Investment (Consolidated)
7	Kansas v. Garcia
8	Rotkiske v. Klemm
9	Mathena v. Malvo
10	Barton v. Barr, Att'y Gen.
11	Kansas v. Glover
12	Citgo Asphalt Refining Co. v. Frescati Shipping Co., LTD.
13	Allen v. Cooper
14	County of Maui, HI v. Hawaii Wildlife Fund
15	Retirement Plans Comm. Of IBM v. Jander
16	Department of Homeland Security v. Regents of Univ. of CA (Consolidated)
17	Hernandez v. Mesa
18	Comcast Corp. v. Nat. Assn. of African American Owned Media
19	Ritzen Group, Inc. v. Jackson Masonry, LLC
20	New York State Rifle & Pistol Assn., Inc. v. City of New York
21	Georgia v. Public.Resource.Org, Inc.
22	Rodriguez v. FDIC
23	Atlantic Richfield Co. v. Christian
24	Intel Corp. Investment Policy Comm. v. Sulyma

(continued)

Number	Case Name
25	*Banister v. Davis*
26	*Guerrero-Lasprilla v. Barr*
27	*Thryv, Inc. v. Click-To-Call Technologies, LP*
28	*Maine Community Health Options v. United States*
29	*Holguin-Hernandez v. United States*
30	*Monasky v. Taglieri*
31	*McKinney v. Arizona*
32	*Lucky Brand Dungarees v. Marcel Fashions Group*
33	*Thole v. U.S. Bank, N.A.*
34	*Kelly v. United States*
35	*Romag Fasteners v. Fossil*
36	*Babb v. Wilkie*
37	*Shular v. United States*
38	*GE Energy Power Conversion France SAS v. Outokumpu Stainless USA*
39	*Espinoza v. Montana Dept. of Revenue*
40	*U.S. Forest Service v. Cowpasture River Assn.*
41	*Opati v. Sudan*
42	*United States v. Sineneng-Smith*
43	*Lomax v. Ortiz-Maequez*
44	*Nasrallah v. Barr, Atty Gen.*
45	*Dept. of Homeland Sec. v. Thuraissigiam*
46	*Seila Law LLC v. Consumer Protection Bureau*
47	*Liu v. SEC*
48	*June Medical Serv. V. Russo, Interim Sec., LA Dept. of Health*
49	*Patent & Trademark v. Booking.com*
50	*USAID v. Alliance for Open Society International, Inc.*
51	*Little Sisters of the Poor v. Pennsylvania*
52	*Barr, Atty Gen v. American Assn. of Political Consultants, Inc.*
53	*McGirt v. Oklahoma*
54	*Our Lady of Guadalupe v. Morrissey-Berru*
55	*Trump v. Mazars/ Trump v. Vance*
56	*Chiafalo v. Washington*
57	*Carney v. Adams*
58	*Texas v. New Mexico*
59	*Rutledge v. Pharmaceutical Care Management Assn.*
60	*Tanzin v. Tanvir*
61	*Google LLC v. Oracle America, Inc.*
62	*Ford Motor Co. v. Montana Eighth Judicial Dist. Court*
63	*United States v. Briggs*
64	*Chicago v. Fulton*
65	*Torres v. Madrid*
66	*Pereida v. Barr*
67	*United States Fish and Wildlife Serv. v. Sierra Club, Inc.*
68	*Salinas v. Railroad Retirement Bd.*
69	*Jones v. Mississippi*
70	*Borden v. United States*
71	*Fulton v. Philadelphia*
72	*Niz-Chavez v. Barr*
73	*Brownback v. King*

(continued)

Number	Case Name
74	*California v. Texas*
75	*Trump v. New York*
76	*Van Buren v. United States*
77	*Nestlé USA, Inc. v. Doe*
78	*CIC Servs., LLC v. IRS*
79	*Edwards v. Vannoy*
80	*Republic of Hungary v. Simon*
81	*Federal Republic of Germany v. Philipp*
82	*Facebook, Inc. v. Duguid*
83	*Harry Schein, Inc. v. Archer & White Sales, Inc.*
84	*Collins v. Mnuchin*
85	*Pham v. Guzman Chavez*
86	*Uzuegbunam v. Preczewski*
87	*AMG Capital Management, LLC v. FTC*
88	*FCC v. Prometheus Radio Project*
89	*BP p.l.c. v. Mayor and City Council of Baltimore*
90	*Florida v. Georgia*
91	*Wilkinson, Acting Atty Gen. v. Dai (Wilkinson, Acting Atty Gen. v. Alcaraz-Enriquez*
92	*Lange v. California*
93	*United States v. Arthrex, Inc.*
94	*Brnovich v. DNC, Arizona Republican Party v. DNC*
95	*Carr v. Saul, Davis v. Saul*
96	*Cedar Point Nursery v. Hassid*
97	*United States v. Cooley*
98	*Caniglia v. Strom*
99	*Goldman Sachs Group v. Arkansas Teacher Retirement Sys.*
100	*Transunion LLC v. Ramirez*
101	*NCAA v. Alston, AAC v. Alston*
102	*Yellen, Sec. of Treasury v. Confederated Tribes of Chehalis Reservation, Alaska Native Village Corp. v. Confederated Tribes of Chehalis Reservation*
103	*Sanchez v. Mayorkas, Sec. of Homeland Security*
104	*Greer v. United States*
105	*United States v. Gary*
106	*City of San Antonio v. Hotels.com, L.P.*
107	*Minerva Surgical, Inc. v. Hologic, Inc.*
108	*Americans for Prosperity v. Bonta, Thomas More Law Center v. Bonta*
109	*Guam v. United States*
110	*Hollyfrontier Cheyenne Refining, LLC. v. Renewable Fuels Assn.*
111	*United States v. Palomar-Santiago*
112	*Mahanoy Area School Dist. v. B.L.*
113	*Penneast Pipeline Co. v. New Jersey*
114	*Mississippi v. Tennessee*
115	*Wooden v. United States*
116	*Brown v. Davenport*
117	*Hemphill v. New York*
118	*United States v. Zubaydah*
119	*Cameron v. EMW Women's Surgical Center*

(continued)

Number	Case Name
120	*Thompson v. Clark*
121	*United States v. Tsarnaev*
122	*Babcock v. Kijakazi*
123	*Whole Woman's Health v. Jackson*
124	*United States v. Texas*
125	*Houston Community College Sys. v. Wilson*
126	*Badgerow v. Walters*
127	*New York State Rifle and Pistol Assn. v. Bruen*
128	*FBI v. Fazaga*
129	*Unicolors, INC. v. H&M Hennes & Mauritz, L. P.*
130	*United States v. Vaello-Madero*
131	*Ramirez v. Collier*
132	*Austin v. Reagan National Advertising*
133	*Becerra v. Empire Health Foundation*
134	*Cummings v. Premier Rehab*
135	*American Hospital Assn. v. Becerra*
136	*Dobbs v. Jackson Women's Health Org.*
137	*Patel v. Garland, Att'y Gen.*
138	*Hughes v. Northwestern University*
139	*United States v. Taylor*
140	*Carson v. Makin*
141	*Shinn v. Ramirez*
142	*Gallardo v. Marstiller*
143	*Johnson v. Arteaga-Martinez*
144	*Garland, Atty Gen. v. Gonzalez*
145	*Boechler, P.C. v. Comm'r of Int. Rev.*
146	*Shurtleff v. Boston*
147	*Cassirer v. Thyssen-Bornemisza Collection*
148	*Federal Election Commission v. Ted Cruz for Senate*
149	*Concepcion v. United States*
150	*Ysleta Del Sur Pueblo v. Texas*
151	*Denezpi v. United States*
152	*Arizona v. San Francisco*
153	*West Virginia v. EPA, North American Coal Corp. v. EPA, Westmoreland Mining Holdings LLC v. EPA, North Dakota v. EPA*
154	*Ruan v. United States, Kahn v. United States*
155	*Marietta Memorial Hospital v. Davita INC.*
156	*Egbert v. Boule*
157	*Morgan v. Sundance, Inc.*
158	*Berger v. North Carolina State Conf. of NAACP*
159	*Golan v. Saada*
160	*ZF Automotive US, Inc. v. Luxshare, LTD., Alixpartners, LLP v. Fund for Protection of Investors' Rights*
161	*Ledure v. Union Pacific Railroad Co.*
162	*Southwest Airlines Co. v. Saxon*
163	*Torres v. Texas Dept of Public Safety*
164	*Viking River Cruises, Inc. v. Moriana*
165	*United States v. Washington*
166	*Siegel v. Fitzgerald*

(continued)

Number	Case Name
167	*George v. McDonough*
168	*Kemp v. United States*
169	*Vega v. Tekoh*
170	*Kennedy v. Bremerton School Dist.*
171	*Nance v. Ward*
172	*Biden v. Texas*
173	*Shoop v. Twyford*
174	*Oklahoma v. Castro-Huerta*

UniqueOutletID: Each print news outlet is assigned its own number.

Number	Media Outlet
1	USA Today
2	The Wall Street Journal
3	The New York Times
4	New York Post
5	Los Angeles Times
6	The Washington Post
7	Star Tribune
8	Newsday
9	Chicago Tribune
10	The Boston Globe
11	NBC News
12	CBS News
13	ABC News
14	Fox News
15	PBS
16	MSNBC
17	CNN
18	Fox Business Network

Case_Name: Full name of the case.

Docket_Number: Docket number of the case.

OASession: This variable separates cases into the sessions of interest.

Number	Session
1	October 7—October 18th, 2019
2	November 4—November 15th, 2019
3	December 2—December 13th, 2019
4	January 13—January 24th, 2020
5	February 24—March 6th, 2020
6	May 4—May 13th, 2020
7	October 5—October 14th, 2020
8	November 2—November 9th, 2020

(continued)

Number	Session
9	November 30—December 9th, 2020
10	January 11—January 19th, 2021
11	February 22—March 3rd, 2021
12	March 22—March 31st, 2021
13	April 19—April 28th, 2021
14	October 4—October 13th, 2021
15	November 1—November 10th, 2021
16	November 29—December 8th, 2021
17	January 10—January 19th, 2022
18	February 21—March 2nd, 2022
19	March 21—March 30th, 2022
20	April 18—April 27th, 2022

News_Outlet: Full name of the news outlet.

StoryNumberforOutlet: How many stories a news outlet produces for each case. For example, if Fox News wrote two articles for the Booking.com case, the first story would be coded a 1 and the second story would be coded a 2. If a news outlet does not produce a story about a case, StoryNumberforOutlet is coded as 0. The purpose of this variable is to match the article quotes to each article.

TelephoneArg: Whether the argument was on a day that the Court argued by telephone. 1 if it was argued by telephone and 0 if it was argued in-person.

DayofOA: Whether the story was released on the day the Court heard oral arguments. 1 if the story was released on the day of oral arguments or 0 if the story was not released on the day of oral arguments.

DayofAudio: Whether the story was released on the Friday the Court released audio. 1 or 0.

Story: Whether the news outlet has a story for a case. 1 if the news outlet has a story and 0 if the news outlet does not have a story.

URL: Full URL of the story.

OriginalStory: Whether it is an original story from the news outlet. An original story is a story that is written by staff members at the news outlet. 1 if it is an original story and 0 if it is not an original story.

NotOriginal: Whether it is not an original story. A not original story is a story that is written by staff members at another news outlet. For example, newspapers like the *Chicago Tribune* tend to take stories from *The New York Times* or the Associated Press. 1 if it is not an original story and 0 if it is an original story.

NewsStory: Whether it is a news story. We define a news story as a description of an event. 1 if it is a news story and 0 if it is not a news story.

OpinionStory: Whether it is an opinion piece. We define an opinion story as someone's opinion about an event. 1 if it is an opinion story and 0 if it is not an opinion story.

BodyContent: Full text content of the news story. We use this variable to pull the quotes from each news story.

BodyWordCount: Word count of the text content included in the BodyContent variable.

QuoteDum: Dichotomous variable for whether the story contains any quotes. 1 if it contains at least 1 quote and 0 if it does not contain any quotes.

QuoteInt: How many quotes the story actually contains from either a justice or an advocate. This takes on an integer value.

AudioClip: Dichotomous variable for whether the story contains an audio clip from OA. 1 if it contains an audio clip and 0 if it does not contain an audio clip.

TotalAlito: How many times Alito was quoted in the story. This takes on an integer value. For example, "this is a bi-state agency," Alito said of the Port Authority, which is led by political appointees from New York and New Jersey. "Why? Why would New Jersey agree to an arrangement like that?" This is one quote and would be coded as 1 because the text in the middle is just providing context. This process will be used for all of the justice and advocate variables below.

TotalSotomayor: How many times Sotomayor was quoted in the story. This takes on an integer value.

TotalThomas: How many times Thomas was quoted in the story. This takes on an integer value.

TotalGinsburg: How many times Ginsburg was quoted in the story. This takes on an integer value.

TotalKavanaugh: How many times Kavanaugh was quoted in the story. This takes on an integer value.

TotalGorsuch: How many times Gorsuch was quoted in the story. This takes on an integer value.

TotalBreyer: How many times Breyer was quoted in the story. This takes on an integer value.

TotalKagan: How many times Kagan was quoted in the story. This takes on an integer value.

TotalRoberts: How many times Roberts was quoted in the story. This takes on an integer value.

TotalBarrett: How many times Barrett was quoted in the story. This takes on an integer value.

AdvocateDum: Whether an advocate is quoted in the story. An advocate is defined as a party's representative. 1 if an advocate is quoted and 0 if an advocate is not quoted.

AdvocateInt: How many quotes are included in the story from advocates in a case. This takes on an integer value.

TotalAdvocatePet: How many quotes are included in the story from the petitioner's advocates in a case. This takes on an integer value.

TotalAdvocateResp: How many quotes are included in the story from the respondent's advocates in a case. This takes on an integer value.

NewQuestioning: Whether the story addresses the new questioning procedure. 1 if it does address the questioning procedure and 0 if it does not address the questioning procedure. The story must address at least one of the following bullet point elements to be labeled a 1:

- The justices cannot interrupt at almost any time with a question
- The justices cannot ask follow-ups to questions from other justices
- The justices cannot jump in with a question that seems more aimed at figuring out the views of the other justices or influencing those views
- Chief Justice John Roberts has the opportunity to ask questions. Then, each of the other justices will have a turn, going in order of seniority
- Chief Justice John Roberts dictates when a justice's turn to interact with an attorney begins and ends.

PhoneOA: Whether the story addresses the new method of OA over the phone including a phrase such as "conference call," "telephone," "livestreamed," "virtual oral argument," and/or "teleconference." This variable takes on the value 1 if it does address the new method of OA. It takes on the value 0 if it does not address the new method of OA.

VARIABLES CODED FOR EACH QUOTE

QuoteWordCount: How many words are in the quote. We only count the words in the quotation marks.

Full: If the quote is at least one full sentence. This variable takes on the value of 1 if the quote is at least one full sentence. It takes on the value of 0 if the quote is not at least one full sentence.

Partial: If the quote is not a complete sentence. This variable takes on the value of 1 if the quote is not at least one full sentence. It takes on the value of 0 if the quote is at least one full sentence.

AdvocateExchange: Whether the quote is said in the story to be a part of an exchange between a justice and an advocate. This variable takes on the value of 1 if it is part of an exchange between a justice and an advocate. It takes on the value of 0 if the quote is not part of an exchange between a justice and an advocate.

JusticeExchange: Whether the quote is said in the story to be a part of an exchange between two or more justices. This variable takes on the value of 1 if it is part of an exchange between a justice and another justice. It takes on the value of 0 if the quote is not part of an exchange between a justice and another justice.

Question: Whether the advocate or justice is quoted for asking a question. 1 or 0. Must include a "?," "asked," or "queried."

CASE-LEVEL DATA

CivLib: Civil Liberties versus Non-Civil Liberties Cases. 1 if it is a civil liberties case and 0 if it is not.

ConCase: Constitutional versus Non-Constitutional Liberties Cases. 1 if it is a constitutional case and 0 if it is not.

StatCase: Statutory versus Non-Statutory Liberties Cases. 1 if it is a statutory case and 0 if it is not.

DSG: Whether the deputy solicitor general is a part of the case. 1 if DSG is a part of the case and 0 if they are not.

SG: Whether the solicitor general is a part of the case. Includes amicus curiae supporting the petitioners or respondent during argument. 1 if the federal government/SG is a part of the case and 0 if they are not.

SGDSG: Whether the deputy solicitor general and/or solicitor general is a part of the case. 1 if they are and 0 if they are not.

Pre-Argument Stories: The number of articles that appear prior to the day of oral argument for each case across three newspapers (*New York Times*, *Los Angeles Times*, and *Washington Post*). This variable takes on an integer value for number of stories from all three news outlets about each case.

TotalTurns: How many turns were taken between the justices during each oral argument.

Appendix

ADDITIONAL TABLES AND MODELS

Table A Logistic Regression of Whether Online Print News Stories Published a Story About an Orally Argued Case (2019–2021 Terms) with May 2020 Session as Reference Category

	Coefficient	Standard Error
Pre-May Sessions	−2.645***	0.226
Post-May Sessions	−2.747***	0.232
Number of Turns	0.014***	0.001
Pre-Argument Stories	0.167***	0.018
Civil Liberties Case	0.096	0.139
Constitutional Case	0.279	0.124
Solicitor General	−0.190	0.127
Constant	−1.596	0.257
Log Likelihood	−1161.659	
Number of Observations	3,132	

Note: May 2020 cases are the reference category.
*p < 0.1; **p < 0.05; ***p < 0.01, two-tailed tests.

Table B Logistic Regression of Whether Online Print News Stories Published a Story About an Orally Argued Case (2019–2021 Terms), Excluding May 2020 Session

	Coefficient	Standard Error
Post-May Sessions	−0.050	0.144
Number of Turns	0.014***	0.001
Pre-Argument Stories	0.186***	0.020
Civil Liberties Case	0.149	0.144
Constitutional Case	0.353*	0.127
Solicitor General	−0.176	0.128
Constant	−4.334***	0.225
Log Likelihood	−1070.557	
Number of Observations	2,989	

Note: Pre-May 2020 cases (before arguments were livestreamed) are the reference category.
*p < 0.1; **p < 0.05; ***p < 0.01, two-tailed tests.

Table C   Logistic Regression of Whether Online Print News Stories Include at Least One Justice Quotation from an Orally Argued Case (2019–2021 Terms) with May 2020 Session as Reference Category

	Coefficient	Standard Error
Pre-May Sessions	−2.375***	0.216
Post-May Sessions	−2.660***	0.226
Number of Turns	0.014***	0.001
Pre-Argument Stories	0.108***	0.013
Civil Liberties Case	0.225	0.145
Constitutional Case	0.212	0.135
Solicitor General	−0.266*	0.143
Constant	−1.810	0.258
Log Likelihood	−1045.583	
Number of Observations	3,132	

Note: May 2020 cases are the reference category.
*p < 0.1; **p < 0.05; ***p < 0.01, two-tailed tests.

Table D   Logistic Regression of Whether Online Print News Stories Include at Least One Justice Quotation from an Orally Argued Case (2019–2021 Terms), Excluding May 2020 Session

	Coefficient	Standard Error
Post-May Sessions	−0.264*	0.149
Number of Turns	0.014***	0.001
Pre-Argument Stories	0.115***	0.014
Civil Liberties Case	0.258*	0.152
Constitutional Case	0.274**	0.139
Solicitor General	−0.243*	0.144
Constant	−4.278***	0.239
Log Likelihood	−948.990	
Number of Observations	2,989	

Note: Pre-May 2020 cases (before arguments were livestreamed) are the reference category.
*p < 0.1; **p < 0.05; ***p < 0.01, two-tailed tests.

Bibliography

Black, Ryan C., and James F. Spriggs. "The Citation and Depreciation of U.S. Supreme Court Precedent." *Journal of Empirical Legal Studies* 10, no. 2 (2013): 325–58.

Black, Ryan C., and Ryan J. Owens. *The Solicitor General and the United States Supreme Court: Executive Branch Influence and Judicial Decisions.* New York: Cambridge University Press, 2012.

Black, Ryan C., and Timothy R. Johnson. "Behind the Velvet Curtain: Understanding Supreme Court Conference Discussions Through the Justices' Conference Notes." *Journal of Appellate Practice and Process* 19, no. 2 (2019): 223–59.

Black, Ryan C., Maron W. Sorenson, and Timothy R. Johnson. "Toward an Actor-Based Measure of Supreme Court Case Salience: Information-Seeking and Engagement During Oral Arguments." *Political Research Quarterly* 66, no. 4 (2013): 804–18.

Black, Ryan C., Ryan J. Owens, and Miles T. Armaly. "A Well-Traveled Lot: A Research Note on Judicial Travel by US Supreme Court Justices." *Justice System Journal* 37, no. 4 (2016): 367–84.

Black, Ryan C., Ryan J. Owens, Justin Wedeking, and Patrick C. Wohlfarth. *U.S. Supreme Court Opinions and Their Audiences.* New York: Cambridge University Press, 2016.

Black, Ryan C., Sarah A. Treul, Timothy R. Johnson, and Jerry Goldman. "Emotions, Oral Arguments, and Supreme Court Decision Making." *The Journal of Politics* 73, no. 2 (April 2011): 572–81.

Black, Ryan C., Timothy R. Johnson, and Justin Wedeking. *Oral Arguments and Coalition Formation on the U.S. Supreme Court.* Ann Arbor: University of Michigan Press, 2012.

Black, Ryan C., Timothy R. Johnson, Ryan J. Owens, and Justin Wedeking. 2023. "Televised Oral Arguments and Judicial Legitimacy: An Initial Assessment." *Political Behavior.* https://doi.org/10.1007/s11109-022-09848-5.

Block, Mervin. *Writing Broadcast News: Shorter, Sharper, Stronger.* Bonus Books, Inc., 1997.

Bryan, Amanda C. "Public Opinion and Setting the Agenda on the U.S. Supreme Court." *American Politics Research* 48, no. 3 (2020): 377–90.

Bryan, Amanda C., and Christopher D. Kromphardt. "Public Opinion, Public Support, and Counter-Attitudinal Voting on the U.S. Supreme Court." *Justice System Journal* 37, no. 4 (2016): 298–317.

Caldeira, Gregory A., and James L. Gibson. "The Etiology of Public Support for the Supreme Court." *American Journal of Political Science* 36, no. 3 (1992): 635–64. https://doi.org/10.2307/2111585.

Carter, E. L. "Supreme Court Oral Argument Video: A Review of Media Effects Research and Suggestions for Study." *Brigham Young University Law Review* 48, no. 6 (2012): 1719–58.

Chaffee, Steven, and Stacey Frank. "How Americans Get Political Information: Print Versus Broadcast News." *The Annals of the American Academy of Political and Social Science* 546, no. 1 (1996): 48–58.

Chen, Qiang, Chen Min, Wei Zhang, Ge Wang, Xiaoyue Ma, and Richard Evans. "Unpacking the Black Box: How to Promote Citizen Engagement through Government Social Media during the COVID-19 Crisis." *Computers in Human Behavior* 110 (2020): 106380.

Clark, Tom S., Jeffrey R. Lax, and Douglas Rice. "Measuring Salience as a Latent Variable." *Law and Courts* 3, no. 1 (2015): 37–65.

Collins, Paul M. "Lobbyists before the U.S. Supreme Court." *Political Research Quarterly* 60, no. 1 (2007): 55–70.

Conway, Bethany A., Kate Kenski, and Di Wang. "The Rise of Twitter in the Political Campaign: Searching for Intermedia Agenda-Setting Effects in the Presidential Primary." *Journal of Computer-Mediated Communication* 20, no. 4 (2015): 363–80.

Corley, Pamela C. "The Supreme Court and Opinion Content: The Influence of Parties' Briefs." *Political Research Quarterly* 61, no. 3 (2008): 468–78.

Davis, Richard. *Decisions and Images: The Supreme Court and the Press.* Prentice Hall, 1994.

Davis, Richard, and Vincent James Strickler. "The Invisible Dance: The Supreme Court and the Press." *Perspectives on Political Science* 29, no. 2 (2000): 85–92.

Dovers, Stephen R., and Adnan A. Hezri. "Institutions and Policy Processes: The Means to the Ends of Adaptation." *WIREs Climate Change* 1, no. 2 (2010): 212–31.

Drok, Nico, and Liesbeth Hermans. "Is There a Future for Slow Journalism? The Perspective of Younger Users." *Journalism Practice* 10, no. 4 (2016): 539–54.

Editorial Board. "Opinion | The Supreme Court Sounds Great. Keep the Broadcasts Coming." *The Washington Post.* WP Company, May 23, 2020. https://www.washingtonpost.com/opinions/the-supreme-court-sounds-great-keep-the-broadcasts-coming/2020/05/22/887895ba-9b04-11ea-89fd-28fb313d1886_story.html.

Ericson, David. "Newspaper Coverage of the Supreme Court: A Case Study." *Journalism Quarterly* 54, no. 3 (1977): 605–7.

Erickson, E. "As The Perpetual News Cycle Goes on Impeachment, Too, Will Soon Be Forgotten." *The Telegraph*, January 26, 2020. https://www.macon.com/opinion/opn-columns-blogs/article239616763.html.

Epstein, Lee, William M. Landes, and Richard A. Posner. "The Best for Last: The Timing of U.S. Supreme Court Decisions." *Duke Law Journal* 64 (March 2015): 991–1022.

Franklin, Robert Arthur. 2005. "McJournalism: The Local Press and the McDonaldization Thesis." In Stuart Allan (editor), Journalism: Critical Issues, Maidenhead: Open University Press, pp. 137–50.

Gibson, James, and Gregory Caldeira. *Citizens, Courts, and Confirmations: Positivity Theory and the Judgments of the American People.* Princeton: Princeton University Press, 2009.

Gibson, James L., and Gregory A. Caldeira. "Confirmation Politics and the Legitimacy of the U.S. Supreme Court: Institutional Loyalty, Positivity Bias, and the Alito Nomination." *American Journal of Political Science* 53, no. 1 (2009): 139–55.

Gibson, James L., Gregory A. Caldeira, and Lester Kenyatta Spence. "Measuring Attitudes toward the United States Supreme Court." *American Journal of Political Science* 47, no. 2 (2003): 354–56.

Golde, Kalvis. "Public Approves of Live Access to Supreme Court Arguments, Polls Show." *SCOTUSblog*, May 21, 2020a. https://www.scotusblog.com/2020/05/public-approves-of-live-access-to-supreme-court-arguments-polls-show/.

Golde, Kalvis. "Senators Ask Supreme Court to Continue with Live Audio." *SCOTUSblog*, May 29, 2020b. https://www.scotusblog.com/2020/05/senators-ask-supreme-court-to-continue-with-live-audio/.

Haider-Markel, Donald P., Mahalley D. Allen, and Morgen Johansen. "Understanding Variations in Media Coverage of U.S. Supreme Court Decisions: Comparing Media Outlets in Their Coverage of Lawrence v. Texas." *Harvard International Journal of Press/Politics* 11, no. 2 (2006): 64–85.

Haltom, William, and Bruce L. Cadwallader. "Reporting on the Courts: How the Mass Media Cover Judicial Actions." *Newspaper Research Journal* 19, no. 4 (1998): 93.

Harder, Raymond A., Julie Sevenans, and Peter Van Aelst. "Intermedia Agenda Setting in the Social Media Age: How Traditional Players Dominate the News Agenda in Election Times." *The International Journal of Press/Politics* 22, no. 3 (2017): 275–93.

Harlan, John M. "What Part Does the Oral Argument Play In the Conduct of an Appeal?" *Cornell Law Quarterly* 41, no. 1 (1955): 6–11.

Heimerl, Florian, Steffen Lohmann, Simon Lange, and Thomas Ertl. "Word Cloud Explorer: Text Analytics Based on Word Clouds." In *2014 47th Hawaii International Conference on System Sciences*, pp. 1833–42. IEEE, 2014.

Hitt, Matthew P., and Kathleen Searles. "Media Coverage and Public Approval of the U.S. Supreme Court." *Political Communication* 35, no. 4 (2018): 566–86.

Hoekstra, Valerie J. *Public Reaction to Supreme Court Decisions.* New York: Cambridge University Press, 2003.

Houston, Rachael, Siyu Li, and Timothy R. Johnson. "Learning to Speak Up: Acclimation Effects and Supreme Court Oral Argument." *Justice System Journal* 42, no. 2 (2021): 115–29.

Houston, Rachael, and Timothy R. Johnson. "Does Greater Transparency Increase Viewership and Engagement? An Analysis of C-SPAN's Live Audio Broadcasts of Supreme Court Oral Argument." *The Year in C-SPAN Archives Research.* Forthcoming 2023.

Howe, Amy. "Courtroom Access: The Nuts and Bolts of Courtroom Seating – and the Lines for Public Access." *SCOTUSblog*, April 9, 2020. https://www.scotusblog .com/2020/04/courtroom-access-the-nuts-and-bolts-of-courtroom-seating-and-the -lines-to-gain-access-to-the-courtroom/.

Jacobi, Tonja, and Matthew Sag. "Taking Laughter Seriously at The Supreme Court." *Vanderbilt Law Review* 72 (2019): 1423–26.

Jacobi, Tonja, and Matthew Sag. "The New Oral Argument: Justices as Advocates." *Notre Dame Law Review* 94 (2019): 1161–76.

Jacobi, Tonja, Timothy R. Johnson, Eve M. Ringsmuth, and Matthew Sag. "Oral Argument in the Time of COVID: The Chief Plays Calvinball." *Southern California Interdisciplinary Law Journal* 30 (2020): 399.

Johnson, Timothy R. *Oral Arguments and Decision Making on the United States Supreme Court.* Albany: State University of New York Press, 2004.

Johnson, Timothy R. "Information, Oral Arguments, and Supreme Court Decision Making." *American Politics Research* 29, no. 4 (2001): 331–51.

Johnson, Timothy R., and Charles Gregory. "The Chief Justice and Oral Arguments at the U.S. Supreme Court." In *The Chief Justice: Appointment and Influence*, edited by Artemus Ward and David Danelski, pp. 151–73. Ann Arbor: University of Michigan Press, 2016.

Johnson, Timothy R., Maron W. Sorenson, Maggie Cleary, and Katie Szarkowicz. "COVID-19 and Supreme Court Oral Argument: The Curious Case of Justice Clarence Thomas." *Journal of Appellate Practice and Process* 21 (2021): 113–62.

Johnson, Timothy R., Paul J. Wahlbeck, and James F. Spriggs. "The Influence of Oral Argument on the U.S. Supreme Court." *American Political Science Review* 100, no. 1 (2006): 99–113.

Johnson, Timothy R., Ryan Black, and Eve M. Ringsmuth. "Hear Me Roar: What Provokes Supreme Court Justices to Dissent from the Bench?" *University of Minnesota Law Review* 93, no. 5 (May 2009): 1560–81.

Johnson, Timothy R., Ryan Black, Jerry Goldman, and Sarah A. Treul. "Inquiring Minds Want to Know: Do Justices Tip Their Hands with Questions at Oral Argument in the U.S. Supreme Court?" *Washington Journal of Law & Policy* 29 (2009): 241–61.

Johnson, Timothy R., Ryan C. Black, and Justin Wedeking. "Pardon the Interruption: An Empirical Analysis of Supreme Court Justices' Behavior During Oral Arguments." *Loyola Law Review* 55 (2009): 331–51.

Johnson, Tyler, and Erica Socker. "Actions, Factions, and Interactions: Newsworthy Influences on Supreme Court Coverage." *Social Science Quarterly* 93, no. 2 (2012): 434–63.

Johnston, C. D., and B. L. Bartels. "Sensationalism and Sobriety Differential Media Exposure and Attitudes toward American Courts." *Public Opinion Quarterly* 74, no. 2 (2010): 260–85.

Joris, Glen, Frederik De Grove, Kristin Van Damme, and Lieven De Marez. "News Diversity Reconsidered: A Systematic Literature Review Unraveling the Diversity in Conceptualizations." *Journalism Studies* 21, no. 13 (2020): 1893–1912.

Knight, Jack. *Institutions and Social Conflict.* New York: Cambridge University Press, 1992.

Krewson, Christopher N. "Save this Honorable Court: Shaping Public Perceptions of the Supreme Court Off the Bench." *Political Research Quarterly* 72, no. 3 (2019): 686–99.

Kromphardt, Christopher D., and Joseph P. Bolton. "Ready for Their Close-Up? Ideological Cues and Strategic Televising in the Ninth Circuit Court of Appeals." *Justice System Journal* 43, no. 3 (2022): 260–78.

LaRowe, Nicholas, and Valerie Hoekstra. "On and Off the Supreme Court Beat: Differences in Newspaper Coverage of the Supreme Court and the Implications for Public Support." In *Covering the United States Supreme Court in the Digital Age,* edited by Richard Davis, pp. 126–52. New York: Cambridge University Press, 2014.

Lee, William E., Daxton R. Stewart, and Jonathan Peters. *The Law of Public Communication.* New York: Routledge, 2020.

Leighley, Jan E. *Mass Media and Politics: A Social Science Perspective.* Houghton Mifflin College Division, 2004.

Li, Siyu, and Tom Pryor. "Humor And Persuasion: The Effects of Laughter during U.S. Supreme Court's Oral Arguments." *Law & Policy* 42, no. 2 (2020): 162–85.

Linos, Katerina, and Kimberly Twist. "The Supreme Court, the Media, and Public Opinion: Comparing Experimental and Observational Methods." *The Journal of Legal Studies* 45, no. 2 (2016): 223–54.

Liptak, Adam. "A Most Inquisitive Court? No Argument There." *The New York Times,* October 7, 2013. https://www.nytimes.com/2013/10/08/us/inquisitive-justices-no-argument-there.html.

Liptak, Adam. "Sotomayor Reflects on First Years on Court." *The New York Times,* February 1, 2011. https://www.nytimes.com/2011/02/01/us/politics/01sotomayor.html.

Lithwick, Dahlia, and Sonja West. "The Supreme Court's Sneaky, Outrageous Reversal on Contraception Coverage." *Slate,* July 4, 2014. https://slate.com/news-and-politics/2014/07/wheaton-college-injunction-the-supreme-court-just-sneakily-reversed-itself-on-hobby-lobby.html.

Livingston, Steven, and W. Lance Bennett. "Gatekeeping, Indexing, and Live-Event News: Is Technology Altering the Construction of News?" *Political Communication* 20, no. 4 (2003): 363–80.

Maltzman, Forrest, James F. Spriggs, and Paul J. Wahlbeck. *Crafting Law on the Supreme Court: The Collegial Game.* New York: Cambridge University Press, 2000.

March, James, and Johan P. Olsen. "Institutional Perspectives on Political Institutions." *Governance: An International Journal of Policy and Administration* 9, no. 3 (1996): 247–64.

Mauro, Tony. "Let the Cameras Roll: Cameras in the Court and the Myth of Supreme Court Exceptionalism." *Reynolds Courts & Media Law Journal* 1 (2011): 259.

Musburger, Robert B. *An Introduction to Writing for Electronic Media: Scriptwriting Essentials Across the Genres.* New York: Routledge, 2012.

North, Douglas C. *Institutions, Institutional Change and Economic Performance.* New York: Cambridge University Press, 1990.

Ornebring, Henrik. "Journalists Thinking about Precarity: Making Sense of the 'New Normal.'" *International Symposium on Online Journalism* 8, no. 1 (2018): 109–27.

Pavlik, J. *Journalism and New Media.* New York: Columbia University Press, 2001.

Perry, Hersel W. *Deciding to Decide: Agenda Setting in the United States Supreme Court.* Cambridge: Harvard University Press, 2009.

Peters, J. "Cold, Wet Wait for Tickets to Supreme Court's Same-Sex Marriage Cases." *The New York Times*, March 25, 2013. https://www.nytimes.com/2013/03/26/us/cold-wet-wait-to-hear-same-sex-marriage-cases.html.

Peters, Jonathan. "The Modern Fight for Media Freedom in the United States." *First Amendment Law Review* 18 (2020): 60–93.

Pottker, Horst. "News and Its Communicative Quality: The Inverted Pyramid—When and Why Did It Appear?." *Journalism Studies* 4, no. 4 (2003): 501–11.

Rehnquist, William R. "Oral Advocacy: A Disappearing Art." *Mercer Law Review* 34 (1984): 1015–25.

Riffe, Daniel. "Scholarly Journals as a Process and Practice Mirror." *Journalism & Mass Communication Educator* 60, no. 2 (2005): 140–44.

Ringsmuth, Eve M., and Timothy R. Johnson. "Supreme Court Oral Arguments and Institutional Maintenance." *American Politics Research* 41, no. 4 (2013): 651–73.

Ritter, Matt. "Intraday Intermedia Agenda-Setting in the Manic World of Online News Reporting." *Southern Communication Journal* 85, no. 4 (2020): 244–53.

Robert, Amanda. "ABA President Calls for Continued Access to Scotus Oral Arguments amid Coronavirus Crisis." *ABA Journal*, 2020. https://www.abajournal.com/news/article/aba-president-calls-for-continued-access-to-supreme-court-oral-arguments.

Roberts, John G. "Oral Advocacy and the Re-Emergence of a Supreme Court Bar." *Journal of Supreme Court History* 30, no. 1 (2005): 68–75.

Rosenberg, H., and C. S. Feldman. *No Time to Think: The Menace of Media Speed and the 24-Hour News Cycle.* A&C Black, 2008.

Schoenherr, Jessica A., and Ryan C. Black. "Friends with Benefits: Case Significance, Amicus Curiae, and Agenda Setting on the U.S. Supreme Court." *International Review of Law and Economics* 58 (2019): 43–53.

Schubert, J. N., S. A. Peterson, G. Schubert, and S. Wasby. "Observing Supreme Court Oral Argument: A Biosocial Approach." *Politics and the Life Sciences* 11, no. 1 (1992): 35–52.

Shah, Dhavan V., Jack M. McLeod, and So-Hyang Yoon. "Communication, Context, and Community: An Exploration of Print, Broadcast, and Internet Influences." *Communication Research* 28, no. 4 (2001): 464–506.

Shullman, Sarah Levien. "The Illusion of Devil's Advocacy: How the Justices of The Supreme Court Foreshadow Their Decisions During Oral Argument." *Journal of Appellate Practice & Process* 6 (2004): 271–73.

Sill, Kaitlyn L., Emily T. Metzgar, and Stella M. Rouse. "Media Coverage of the U.S. Supreme Court: How Do Journalists Assess the Importance of Court Decisions?" *Political Communication* 30, no. 1 (2013): 58–80.

Slotnik, E. E., and J. A. Segal. *Television News and the Supreme Court: All the News That's Fit to Air?* New York: Cambridge University Press, 1998.

Spaeth, Harold J., Lee Epstein, Andrew D. Martin, Jeffrey A. Segal, Theodore J. Ruger, and Sara C. Benesh. The Supreme Court Judicial Database, 2022. http://Supremecourtdatabase.org/.

Spill, R. L., and Z. M. Oxley. "Philosopher Kings or Political Actors-How the Media Portray the Supreme Court." *Judicature* 87, no. 1 (2003): 22–87.

Standaert, Willem, Steve Muylle, and Amit Basu. "Business Meetings in a Postpandemic World: When and How to Meet Virtually." *Business Horizons* 65, no. 3 (2022): 267–75.

Sullivan, Barry, and Megan M. Canty. "Interruptions in Search of a Purpose: Oral Argument in the Supreme Court, October Terms 1958–60 and 2010–12." *Utah Law Review*, 2015, no. 5 (2015): 1005–82.

Thorp-Lancaster, D. "Microsoft Teams Hits 75 Million Daily Active Users, Up from 44 Million in March." *Windows Central* (2020). https://www.windowscentral.com/microsoft-teams-hits-75-million-daily-active-users.

Vargo, Chris J., Lei Guo, and Michelle A. Amazeen. "The Agenda-Setting Power of Fake News: A Big Data Analysis of the Online Media Landscape from 2014 to 2016." *New Media & Society* 20, no. 5 (2018): 2028–49.

Vasterman, Peter L. "Media-Hype: Self-Reinforcing News Waves, Journalistic Standards and the Construction of Social Problems." *European Journal of Communication* 20, no. 4 (2005): 508–30.

Vonbun, Ramona, Katharina Kleinen-von Königslöw, and Klaus Schoenbach. "Intermedia Agenda-Setting in a Multimedia News Environment." *Journalism* 17, no. 8 (2016): 1054–73.

Wahlbeck, Paul J., James F. Spriggs, and Forrest Maltzman. "Marshalling the Court: Bargaining and Accommodation on the United States Supreme Court." *American Journal of Political Science* 42, no. 1 (1998): 294–315.

Wasby, Stephen L., Anthony A. D'Amato, and Rosemary Metrailer. "The Functions of Oral Argument in the U.S. Supreme Court." *Quarterly Journal of Speech* 62, no. 4 (1976): 410–22.

Weaver, David, and Lars Willnat. "Journalists in the 21st Century: Conclusions." In *The Global Journalist in the 21st Century*, edited by David Weaver and Lars Willnat, pp. 539–62. Routledge, 2012.

Wedeking, Justin, and Michael A. Zilis. "Disagreeable Rhetoric and the Prospect of Public Opposition: Opinion Moderation on the US Supreme Court." *Political Research Quarterly* 71, no. 2 (2022): 380–94.

Woodward, Bob, and Scott Armstrong. *The Brethren: Inside the Supreme Court.* New York: Simon & Schuster, 2005.

Yopp, Jan Johnson, Katherine C. McAdams, and Ryan Thornburg. *Reaching Audiences: A Guide to Media Writing.* Pearson Allyn and Bacon, 2007.

Zamith, R., and J. A. Braun. "Technology and Journalism." In *The International Encyclopedia of Journalism Studies*, edited by Tim P. Vos, Folker Hanusch, Dimitra Dimitrakopoulou, Margaretha Geertsema-Sligh, and Annika Sehl. John Wiley & Sons, Inc., 2019. DOI: 10.1002/9781118841570.iejs0040.

Zilis, Michael A. *The Limits of Legitimacy.* Ann Arbor: University of Michigan Press, 2015.

Notes

INTRODUCTION

1. For information about oral arguments, see https://www.supremecourt.gov/oral_arguments/oral_arguments.aspx (last accessed December 30, 2022). The importance of this cannot be understated. Indeed, while members of the press and a lucky few from the public who obtain seats in the courtroom experience arguments in real time, space is quite limited (see, e.g., https://www.supremecourt.gov/oral_arguments/courtroomseating.aspx, last accessed December 30, 2022). We discuss this at length below.

2. During the 1918 Spanish flu pandemic, the justices postponed arguments for a month. However, the technology did not then exist to hold remote arguments (see, e.g., https://www.scotusblog.com/2020/04/courtroom-access-faced-with-a-pandemic-the-supreme-court-pivots/, last accessed December 30, 2022).

3. https://www.supremecourt.gov/ (last accessed December 30, 2022).

4. https://www.supremecourt.gov/publicinfo/press/pressreleases/pr_09-28-22 (last accessed December 30, 2022).

5. We discuss this process in more detail under the section "Evolving Access to Supreme Court Oral Arguments."

6. The Court's term starts on the first Monday of every October and runs through late June or early July the following year. When a case is particularly high profile, the Court sometimes released audio of the proceedings the same day as the arguments. See, e.g., *Bush v. Gore* (2000), *Citizens United v. FEC* (2010), and *NFIB v. Sebelius* (2012).

7. https://www.supremecourt.gov/publicinfo/press/pressreleases/pr_09-28-10 (last accessed December 30, 2022).

8. https://www.supremecourt.gov/oral_arguments/argument_audio/2021 (last accessed December 30, 2022).

9. Throughout the book we use, interchangeably, the terms *volume* and *frequency*.

10. This covers the months October 2019 through April 2022.

11. However, as we note above, October 2021 was the first time the Court provided real-time audio for in-person hearings. It announced its plan to continue to offer a live audio feed of the arguments taking place, through its final argument session in April 2022, and extended this practice for the October 2022 Term that runs through June 2023.

12. See fixthecourt.com (last accessed December 30, 2022). To understand more about the Supreme Court Bar, navigate to: https://www.supremecourt.gov/filingandrules/supremecourtbar.aspx (last accessed December 20, 2022).

13. See https://vtdigger.org/2019/03/21/sen-leahy-introduces-bill-allow-cameras-federal-courts/ (last accessed December 30, 2022). They have penned such letters in the past as well. Further, as late as June 2021, a panel in the US Senate approved a bill requiring cameras for Supreme Court oral arguments (see, e.g., https://www.forbes.com/sites/andrewsolender/2021/06/24/senate-panel-approves -bill-requiring-tv-cameras-in-supreme-court/?sh=378a229f1a6c, last accessed December 30, 2022).

14. For example, state and local governments have faced the challenge of complying with open meeting laws during the pandemic (see, e.g., https://www.claremoreprogress.com/news/pandemic-redefines-public-access-to-government-meetings /article_62403fa4-85d4-11eb-a149-2bb6387acae2.html, last accessed December 30, 2022).

15. This is not to say justices are fully out of the public eye. In fact, Krewson (2019) and Black et al. (2016) demonstrate they engage in a wide variety of public relations events especially when they can control the narrative—such as giving talks—as Justice Amy Coney Barrett did when she tried to keep the press from attending a 2021 McConnell Center event where she was speaking (see https://fixthecourt .com/2021/10/barretts-chambers-refused-allow-livestreaming-video-mcconnell-center-event/, last accessed December 30, 2022).

We also know the justices often work closely with a pool of journalists who write stories or full biographies profiling them (e.g., Adam Liptak at the *New York Times*, Nina Totenberg at *National Public Radio*, and Joan Biskupic at CNN). Note that a key reason for keeping cameras from the courtroom (see, e.g., Black 2022) is that the justices worry about what happens when media coverage goes beyond what they can control. In short, the justices are open to being in the public eye but always have a penchant for wanting to control the narrative when they do—something that is less possible with livestreamed audio or, in the future, livestreamed video.

16. See https://www.msnbc.com/rachel-maddow-show/expensive-seat-the -supreme-court-msna583941 (last accessed December 30, 2022).

17. See https://www.scotusblog.com/2020/04/courtroom-access-the-nuts-and -bolts-of-courtroom-seating-and-the-lines-to-gain-access-to-the-courtroom/ (last accessed December 20, 2022). The scarcity of seats has spawned a secretive, informal economy of paid line-standers. See https://www.cnbc.com/2019/02/25/paid-line -standers-waiting-for-supreme-court-arguments-over-wwi-cross.html (last accessed December 30, 2022).

18. The twenty-four-hour cycle traditionally applied to television news channels (Pavlik 2001). However, online journalists have borrowed techniques from the broadcasting industry in their efforts to also provide news coverage "around the clock." This has ultimately led to the same twenty-four-hour news cycle for online print news outlets (Rosenberg and Feldman 2008).

19. The following outlets hold press passes that allow one of their reporters to attend oral arguments: ABC, CBS, CNN, Fox News, *L.A. Times*, NBC News, *The New York Times*, *USA Today*, *Wall Street Journal*, and *The Washington Post*.

20. As with the subject of this book, inaugural activities were significantly scaled back in January 2021 due to the ongoing pandemic. https://www.voanews.com/a/2020-usa-votes_biden-plans-scaled-back-inauguration-avoid-spreading-coronavirus-crowds/6199194.html (last accessed December 30, 2022).

21. Note that Supreme Court Terms typically begin in October and end in April and are referred to by the year in which they commence. Thus the 2022 Term began in October 2022 and concludes in May 2022.

22. See, generally, Argument Transcripts, SUP. CT. OF THE US, https://www.supremecourt.gov/oral_arguments/argument_transcript/2019 (last accessed December 30, 2022).

23. https://www.supremecourt.gov/publicinfo/press/pressreleases/pr_03-16-20 (last accessed December 30, 2022).

24. https://www.supremecourt.gov/publicinfo/press/pressreleases/pr_04-28-20 (last accessed December 30, 2022).

25. https://www.supremecourt.gov/publicinfo/press/pressreleases/pr_04-30-20 (last accessed December 30, 2022).

26. https://www.supremecourt.gov/oral_arguments/calendarsandlists.aspx (last accessed December 30, 2022).

27. The US House of Representatives and the US Senate offer "Floor Webcasts." From January 2021 to January 2022 Congress will be in session for 166 days. That is 166 days for the public to see members in action compared to the Supreme Court, which is only in front of the public during oral arguments for roughly a third of the time, see https://history.house.gov/Institution/Session-Dates/110-Current/ (last accessed December 30, 2022).

28. Admittedly, the release pertained to only ten cases but this was well beyond anything the Court had ever done in terms of same-day release of argument audio.

29. The reason for this change is attributable to the arguments held for the landmark case *Bush v. Gore* (2000) which focused on recounting Florida votes to determine which presidential candidate would win the state's electoral votes.

30. For the most part, the Supreme Court has made its own rules. For a review of the Court and its procedures, see https://www.supremecourt.gov/about/procedures.aspx (last accessed December 30, 2022).

31. Oftentimes same-day release would come after requests or pressure from the media or Court watchers, including scholars. For example, there was pressure for the justices to release same day audio of the health care cases in 2012 (over the constitutionality of Obamacare). On March 16 of that year, National Public Radio reported on

such pressure—https://www.npr.org/2012/03/16/148774081/supreme-court-allows
-same-day-audio-in-healthcare-case (last accessed December 30, 2022).

32. https://www.supremecourt.gov/publicinfo/press/pressreleases/pr_09-14-06
(last accessed December 30, 2022).

33. https://www.supremecourt.gov/publicinfo/press/pressreleases/pr_09-28-10
(last accessed December 30, 2022).

34. See, e.g., https://lawblog.justia.com/2010/10/05/supreme-court-releasing-audio
-but-not-ready-for-prime-time/ (last accessed December 30, 2022).

35. But even then, reporters could not record arguments. For a full description of
the Court's move toward greater access, prior to May 2020, see: https://www.suprem-
ecourt.gov/oral_arguments/availabilityoforalargumenttranscripts.aspx (last accessed
December 30, 2022).

36. *Supreme Court Visitors Film* (C-SPAN television broadcast Feb. 16, 1998),
https://www.c-span.org/video/?100767-1/supreme-court-visitors-film (last accessed
December 30, 2022).

37. www.c-span.org/video/?2514-1/upcoming-pbs-program-supreme-court (discussing PBS Special, *This Honorable Court*) (last accessed December 30, 2022).

38. www.c-span.org/video/?2514-1/upcoming-pbs-program-supreme-court (discussing PBS Special, *The Honorable Court*) (last accessed December 30, 2022).

39. Although the justices also announce their decisions, once made, in open court
(Johnson et al. 2009).

40. For a rare glimpse of a behind-the-scenes account of Supreme Court decision
making, see, for example, Woodward and Armstrong (2005).

41. It is difficult to measure the lifespan of news stories because it is largely
dependent on the topic area (politics and elections, social issues, environment, etc.)
and how lifespan is measured (readership, distribution, etc.). Additionally, news
stories can have multiple lifespans. However, "The Lifespan of News Stories" offers
a unique approach by depicting this concept using Google Trends API (see https://
www.newslifespan.com/, last accessed December 30, 2022). It quantifies the evolution of search interest across a sixty-day window surrounding each event. According
to their calculations, most politics and elections stories have a lifespan of zero to
one day.

42. Of course, we cannot fully disentangle the fact that other parts of the new procedures (the justices being called on by the chief justice to speak in order of seniority
or the arguments happening on the phone) may also contribute to coverage (see, e.g.,
Jacobi et al. 2021). That said, it is the livestreaming that is the key procedural change
with respect to news media access to the Court, which could impact the nature of
coverage.

43. Though SCOTUS blog provides timely and thorough coverage of the Court
and its proceedings, including liveblogs, its audience is a niche group of people who
are quite attentive to the Supreme Court. The news outlets we examine, including
USA Today, *The New York Times*, and CNN, all reach much broader audiences of
people who are not specifically seeking out coverage of the Court.

CHAPTER 1

1. See https://thebolditalic.com/friday-5-virtual-dance-parties-that-will-make-you-happy-aa9aea19b33c (last accessed December 30, 2022).

2. https://www.ajmc.com/view/a-timeline-of-covid19-developments-in-2020 (last accessed December 30, 2022).

3. It is likely that the use of videoconferencing will continue long after the pandemic ends. In fact, Gartner predicts that only 25 percent of business meetings will take place in-person by 2024 (Standaert et al. 2021).

4. Roughly eight-in-ten Americans (81 percent) say they have talked with others via video calls since the beginning of the pandemic. See https://www.pewresearch.org/internet/2021/09/01/how-the-internet-and-technology-shaped-americans-personal-experiences-amid-covid-19/ (last accessed December 30, 2022).

5. As an aside, the US Supreme Court argues that even during times of crisis, when the government has not declared martial law, citizens must have access to civilian courts—*Ex Parte Milligan* (1866).

6. https://www.uscourts.gov/news/2020/03/31/judiciary-authorizes-videoaudio-access-during-covid-19-pandemic (last accessed December 30, 2022).

7. https://www.uscourts.gov/news/2021/02/18/pandemic-lingers-courts-lean-virtual-technology (last accessed December 30, 2022).

8. https://www.supremecourt.gov/publicinfo/press/pressreleases/pr_03-16-20 (last accessed December 30, 2022).

9. One political scientist (Professor Jessica Schoenherr, University of South Carolina—jaschoenherr.com) even told us she listened to a case while out on her daily run!

10. Data do not exist on the number of gallery members who usually attend arguments in-person but given the limited number of available seats we do know many fewer watched them, than currently listen to livestreamed arguments (see, e.g., Houston and Johnson forthcoming 2023).

11. A session, or sitting, refers to all the arguments in one month of a given term. Thus, there is a monthly sitting that usually takes place over the course of two weeks. For example, during its 2022 Term, the justices had a session/sitting that ran from November 28 to December 7. Readers can navigate to https://www.supremecourt.gov/oral_arguments/calendarsandlists.aspx to see the cases argued during each session in our dataset (last accessed December 30, 2022).

12. To gather this list, we utilized Cision: https://www.cision.com/2019/01/top-ten-us-daily-newspapers/ (last accessed December 30, 2022). As of 2022, this list remains the same. The following outlets in our data have press passes that allow one of their reporters to attend oral arguments: ABC, CBS, CNN, Fox News, *L.A. Times*, NBC News, *The New York Times*, *USA Today*, *Wall Street Journal*, and *The Washington Post*. This means the *New York Post*, *Star Tribune*, *Newsday*, *Chicago Tribune*, *The Boston Globe*, PBS, MSNBC, and Fox Business Network do not hold press passes. Unsurprisingly, the news outlets that have press passes produced more stories

on average than outlets without press passes. For a full list of organizations with press passes during the years encompassed by our dataset, see: https://www.supremecourt.gov/publicinfo/Hard_Pass_List_OT_21.pdf, https://www.supremecourt.gov/publicinfo/Hard_Pass_List_OT_20.pdf, and https://www.supremecourt.gov/publicinfo/Hard_Pass_List_OT_19.pdf (each last accessed December 30, 2022).

13. Our analysis does not assess media outlets that report exclusively on politics or the Supreme Court (i.e., The Hill, Politico, SCOTUSBlog.com) because we are interested in television and newspaper news outlets that reach broad public audiences. Future research should consider how these other types of news outlets report on the Court's oral arguments.

14. According to their website, the Media Bias Chart calculates overall news source scores based on scores of individual articles (in the case of online news sources) or episodes (in the cases of podcasts, radio, TV, and video-based sources). Each individual article and episode are rated by at least three human analysts with balanced right, left, and center self-reported political viewpoints. That is, at least one person who has rated the article self-identifies as being right-leaning, one as center, and one as left-leaning. Currently, human analysts are given randomized articles during live shifts (on Zoom). They do not see the source of each news story, only the content. See https://adfontesmedia.com/how-ad-fontes-ranks-news-sources/ (last accessed November 7, 2022).

15. See https://www.pewresearch.org/journalism/fact-sheet/newspapers/ (last accessed December 30, 2022).

16. See https://www.pewresearch.org/journalism/fact-sheet/news-platform-fact-sheet/ (last accessed December 30, 2022). In the same poll, Pew also finds that across digital platforms, people prefer news websites or apps over social media and podcasts.

17. See https://www.pewresearch.org/fact-tank/2021/01/12/more-than-eight-in-ten-americans-get-news-from-digital-devices/ (last accessed December 30, 2022).

18. Our coding decision is based on the traditional twenty-four-hour news cycle, which has become even shorter with the advent of digital media (see our discussion of news cycles in the Introduction).

19. This codebook is available in the Appendix.

20. For this study, we only analyze quotes that come directly from the oral argument sessions. We do not analyze quotes in the articles and stories that come from the case briefs filed by the parties or by *amicus curiae* (friend of the Court) briefs.

21. The exchange variables are only coded if the RAs could explicitly determine from the story that it was a part of an exchange. Otherwise, these were left as missing values.

22. This case overturned the Court's abortion rights precedent set in *Roe v. Wade* (1973): https://www.cnn.com/2021/12/01/politics/supreme-court-roe-v-wade-oral-arguments/index.html (last accessed December 30, 2022).

23. Radio and print publications come in third and fourth. Only 7 percent of people prefer radio and only 5 percent prefer print. See https://www.pewresearch.org/journalism/fact-sheet/news-platform-fact-sheet/ (last accessed December 30, 2022).

24. Note that LNA is behind a paywall. For the original broadcast transcripts, and data we collected from them, please contact the authors. We will gladly provide any and all replication data.

25. We ultimately excluded Fox Business broadcast news coverage from our dataset because, after an exhaustive search, we could not find their story transcripts. However, Fox Business is in our online print media dataset.

26. Lexis Nexis Academic search results for CNN Broadcast Transcript Reporting Clarence Thomas Speaking in *Brown v. Davenport* (2022) and *Hemphill v. New York* (2022), from October 5, 2021 (source: Lexis Nexis Academic Database accessed through the University of Minnesota. Data available from authors upon request).

27. See https://transcripts.cnn.com/show/ip/date/2021-10-05/segment/02.

28. Excerpt of Original Broadcast Transcript from CNN that Reports on Clarence Thomas Speaking in *Brown v. Davenport* (2022) and *Hemphill v. New York* (2022), from October 5, 2021. "Johnson & Johnson Asks FDA To Authorize Booster Shots; Sen. Mike Braun (R-IN) Is Interviewed About Debt Limit; Soon: Biden Arrives In Michigan To Pitch Economic Agenda." Aired 12:30-1p ET (source: Lexis Nexis Academic Database accessed through the University of Minnesota. Data available from authors upon request).

29. Clark, Lax, and Rice (2014) measure Latent Salience as

"the number of stories about a case in each paper—distinguishing among stories about the decision to hear the Supreme Court case i.e., grant certiorari, stories about oral argument, stories about pending cases, and stories about the final decision." In so doing, they specify "a latent variable model which includes a Poisson random variable, a count variable with a rate parameter that is a function of the latent salience of the case, as well as stage-, newspaper-, and term-specific intercepts" (45).

For our purposes, however, we cannot rely on this model because we are only concerned with stories that were written prior to oral argument. This means that we do not collect stories about oral argument, stories about pending cases (unless they happened prior to oral argument), and stories about the final decision to assess pre-argument salience. For this reason, we instead collect these data and analyze them as a count variable. That is, we simply capture how many stories were written about each case prior to oral argument from the three newspapers Clark, Lax, and Rice (2014) rely on for their analysis.

CHAPTER 2

1. https://www.opm.gov/policy-data-oversight/pay-leave/pay-administration/fact-sheets/holidays-work-schedules-and-pay/ (last accessed December 20, 2022).

2. These include Election Day, Susan B. Anthony Day, and Cesar E. Chavez Day. https://constitutioncenter.org/blog/five-other-days-that-could-be-proposed-as-federal-holidays (last accessed December 20, 2022).

3. That said, one of the coauthors on this book (Johnson), and avowed Court Geek, regularly posts on Facebook about his excitement for the First Monday in October. In fact, on October 4, 2021, he declared that this day should be celebrated:

"Happy First Monday in October. It really should be a national holiday. This term is gonna be a doozy!" https://www.facebook.com/timothy.r.johnson.376/posts/pfbid03 WQV4LeeLjLCkJ1JjpTR7q2AqtstH8bPvoZqkezQSgHzymsWrDu5aUzkiMXJjbrgl (last accessed December 20, 2022).

4. For example, since 2018, *The New York Times* averaged more than three stories about the new term in the weeks surrounding the First Monday (defined as September 15 to October 15). Note, however, that in both 2018 and 2020 there were many more articles (that we do not include in our count) about the confirmation battles for Justices Brett Kavanaugh (2018) and Amy Coney Barrett (2020). In terms of viewership of the first argument session, the Court has had two First Mondays since livestreaming began. For these argument days, C-SPAN averaged more than 6,200 viewers—well above the average viewership for other argument days during these terms. While these data are only suggestive, they do indicate many people flock to C-SPAN's website to listen to the nation's opaquest federal institution when it begins its work each year (all data for this footnote gathered by the authors). https:// www.c-span.org/search/?sdate=&edate=&searchtype=Videos&sort=Most+Recent +Event&text=0&sponsorid%5B%5D=1133&formatid%5B%5D=33 (last accessed December 20, 2022).

5. https://www.cspan.org/search/?sdate=05%2F04%2F2020&edate=05%2F04 %2F2020&congressSelect=&yearSelect=&searchtype=Videos&sort=Most+Recent +Event&text=0&sponsorid%5B%5D=1133&formatid%5B%5D=33 (last accessed December 20, 2022).

6. These included, as we discuss below, cases involving the clash between religious freedom and the Obamacare provision on insurance coverage for contraceptives, subpoenas to obtain documents from the Trump administration, presidential immunity from the criminal process while in office, and the electoral college.

7. We do not distinguish between telephonic livestreamed cases (October Term 2020) and in-person cases that were simultaneously livestreamed (October Term 2021).

8. In Livingston and Bennett's language, livestreaming tore down the technology gate of their gatekeeping model.

9. Unsurprisingly, because it was the first case to ever be livestreamed, *Patent & Trademark v. Booking.com* (2020) received the most coverage. Specifically, it garnered twenty-seven online print media articles across the outlets we analyze.

10. Of course, this initial spike, and then return to normal, could also be explained by the fact that, beyond the pandemic, little was happening during May 2020. Thus, it could be that the Court was the only game in town (literally) to listen to, analyze, and discuss. While we cannot rule out this possibility with respect to coverage in the short term, the evidence persuasively indicates that access to livestreamed audio did not prompt online print media outlets to make long-term changes in the volume of their coverage.

11. https://adfontesmedia.com/interactive-media-bias-chart/ (last accessed December 20, 2022). Remember that our liberal online print media outlets include the *New York Times*, the *Los Angeles Times*, *the Washington Post*, the *Boston Globe*, NBC News, MSNBC, and CNN. Our conservative outlets include the *New York Post*, Fox News, and Fox Business News. Finally, our centrist outlets are *USA*

Today, The Wall Street Journal, the *Star Tribune, Newsday,* the *Chicago Tribune,* ABC News, CBS News, and PBS. Recall, also, that this analysis only includes the online print stories from these sources. For an analysis of broadcast stories, see chapter 4.

12. We note that it looks as though there was much less conservative coverage across all sessions in our sample. This is an artifact of the fact that only three of the eighteen media outlets in our dataset are considered conservative according to the Media Bias Chart. See https://adfontesmedia.com/interactive-media-bias-chart/ (last accessed December 30, 2022). Of course, we would like to have had an equal number of outlets across the ideological spectrum, but our decision rule was to focus on the top outlets based on circulation rather than based on ideological predisposition.

13. Logistic regression is the most common discrete choice model for binary outcomes. As in linear regression, some function of subjects' scores on the independent variables is used to make predictions about their dependent variable scores. But we are predicting their probability of being in one group or the other of a categorical dependent variable, not a continuous dependent variable score. In other words, we are trying to make predictions about the probability of a particular outcome – whether an article appears about a given argument or not. This suits our needs, as we want to make predictions about whether a media outlet does or does not have at least one story rather than about the number of stories that appear.

14. For a full description of the Clark et al. variable, please see their coding scheme (2014).

15. Amicus curiae translates to Friend of the Court and is a way for groups who are not a party to the case to have their voice heard by the justices (see, e.g., Black and Owens 2012).

16. We run this model in several different ways. First, we change May 2020 to the reference category (i.e., dummy for Pre-May and dummy for Post-May Sessions). We find that when May is the reference category, both pre-May and post-May coverage are significantly lower in terms of the likelihood of an outlet producing a story. This also supports the conclusion that May 2020 is an anomaly for frequency of news media coverage. We also run the model by removing the May 2020 session entirely. We find that the Post-May Sessions variable is not statistically significant, which suggests that this finding holds when the May session is included or excluded in the modeling. See table A and table B in the appendix.

CHAPTER 3

1. https://www.cnn.com/2020/05/04/politics/clarence-thomas-question/index.html (last accessed December 20, 2022).

2. Oral argument audio. *Patent and Trademark Office v. Booking.com B.V.,* Docket 19-4619-46 (2020). https://www.supremecourt.gov/oral_arguments/audio/2019/19-46 (last accessed December 20, 2022).

3. Oral argument audio. *Patent and Trademark Office v. Booking.com B.V.*, Docket 19-4619-46 (2020). https://www.supremecourt.gov/oral_arguments/audio /2019/19-46 (last accessed December 20, 2022).

4. See note 11 in chapter 1 for a definition of an argument session.

5. This is often touted as the main concern justices have for why they are so opposed to having cameras in the courtroom for oral arguments. That is, they believe they will be quoted out of context and that could harm the Court's legitimacy (see, e.g., Black et al. 2023).

6. An original story is one written by staff members at the news outlet that publishes it. A story we do not consider original is one that appears in an outlet but that was written by staff members at another news outlet and then reprinted. For example, newspapers like the *Chicago Tribune* often take stories from the *New York Times* or the *Associated Press* and credit the original source.

7. Note the gaps in Justices Amy Coney Barrett and Ginsburg panels occur because Ginsburg died in September 2020 and Barrett ascended the bench a month later in October 2020. Otherwise, a single justice was absent only rarely from oral argument and not for lengthy periods during the sessions in our sample (data available from the authors upon request).

8. As we note in chapter 2, the Court heard ten cases during the May 2020 oral argument sitting. *Trump v. Mazars* (2020) and *Trump v. Vance* (2020), along with *Chiafalo v. Washington* (2020) and *Colorado Dept. of State v. Baca* (2020), were argued on the same day and covered together by the news media.

9. The next closest sitting is the January 2020 session that has three out of eight cases on the list.

10. In our modeling for both frequency of stories in chapter 2 and frequency of quotes in this chapter, we include stories and quotes from original and reprinted stories. We do this because we are interested in general coverage from the eighteen media outlets in our dataset. In this particular section, however, we distinguish between the two types of stories because we are curious to what extent news outlets have the resources to write their own stories as opposed to getting their stories from a newswire.

11. A newswire distributes news to editorial offices and journalists in news agencies. The purpose of this arrangement is so that news agencies do not have to hire reporters for every issue area; newswires cover the gaps in coverage for agencies. Rather than having a reporter who focuses on the Supreme Court exclusively, for instance, the *Star Tribune* may purchase a story about a Supreme Court argument from the *Associated Press*, a well-known newswire, instead.

12. In chapter 1 we discuss, in much greater detail, the resources required to provide original coverage.

13. We again run this model several different ways. First, we change May 2020 to the reference category (i.e., dummy for Pre-May and dummy for Post-May Sessions). Like the findings in chapter 2, we find here that when May is the reference category, both pre-May and post-May coverage are significantly lower in terms of the likelihood of an outlet including a quote in a story. We also run the model by removing the May 2020 session entirely. We find that the Post-May Sessions variable is statistically

significant at the p < 0.1 level when the Pre-May Session is the reference category. However, it is a negative coefficient which suggests that compared to the Pre-May Sessions, there were fewer quotes included in stories after the initial May 2020 Session. See table C and table D in the Appendix.

CHAPTER 4

1. https://www.bls.gov/tus/ (last accessed December 30, 2022).

2. https://www.bls.gov/tus/ (last accessed December 30, 2022).

3. Remember that we omit Fox Business Network from our broadcast analysis because transcripts of its broadcasts are not available through LexisNexis Academic's database.

4. Chapter 1 reviews such distinctions, and we also do so below in the section titled *Nature of Broadcast News Coverage*.

5. See chapter 1, note 14.

6. https://adfontesmedia.com/interactive-media-bias-chart/ (last accessed December 16, 2022).

7. We are not comparing media outlets by ideological coverage to each other because the outlets are not equally proportioned across all three categories. As we describe in chapter 1, there are three center outlets, one conservative outlet, and three liberal outlets that produced broadcast stories.

8. Due to the paucity of data on broadcast coverage of arguments, we do not offer generalizable models of this relationship. However, the data used here provide support for our expectation that news media coverage would not be substantially altered by access to livestreamed oral audio in the long term.

9. According to Musburger (2012), broadcast reporters may only have fifteen to thirty seconds to tell a story. "Every item in broadcasting must be timed to the maximum of each story's allotted time in the typical newscast, which airs approximately 22 minutes of actual news. Two ways of accomplishing this are either through unusual phrasing or by loading the first line with facts" (Musburger 2012, 98). The inverted triangle of print reporting is not necessarily followed. For more information about the inverted triangle, see Pottker (2003).

10. For the full story navigate to: https://www.foxnews.com/politics/supreme-court-tips-off-a-legal-fight-over-ncaa-amateurism-restrictions (last accessed December 30, 2022).

11. For these full stories, and all others used in this chapter, please contact us directly.

12. We continue to use the number of online print stories before oral argument as the pre-argument salience measure. While there could be some disconnect here between print and broadcast, we use this approach because very few pre-argument broadcast stories were available.

13. CNN Broadcast Coverage of *California v. Texas* (2021). Story from October 13, 2020. (Source: Lexis Nexis Academic Database accessed through the University of Minnesota. Data available from authors upon request.)

14. Because of the differences between broadcast and online print that we describe above, we continue this section by homing in on broadcast coverage exclusively. Additionally, we take a more qualitative approach here with these broadcast data.

15. See, for instance, Johnson, Timothy R., Maron Sorenson, Maggie Cleary, and Katie Szarkowicz. 2021. "COVID-19 and Supreme Court Oral Argument: The Curious Case of Justice Clarence Thomas." *Journal of Appellate Practice and Process.* Vol 21. #1: 113–162.

16. This is akin to the political science literature that uses oral arguments to predict case outcomes (see, e.g., Johnson et al. 2009; Black et al. 2011).

17. According to Heimerl et al. (2014, 1833), "Word clouds have emerged as a straightforward and visually appealing visualization method for text. They are used in various contexts as a means to provide an overview by distilling text down to those words that appear with highest frequency."

CONCLUSION

1. https://www.theguardian.com/law/2020/may/04/supreme-court-livestream -arguments-telphone (last accessed December 19, 2022).

2. https://www.usatoday.com/story/news/politics/2020/05/04/supreme-court -hears-first-ever-oral-argument-phone-live-audio/3077073001/ (last accessed December 19, 2022).

3. https://www.washingtonpost.com/opinions/2022/10/02/supreme-court-audio -broadcasts-cameras-video/ (last accessed December 19, 2022).

4. https://fixthecourt.com/wp-content/uploads/2022/03/Practitioners-live-audio -letter.pdf (last accessed December 31, 2022).

5. Testimony before a House Appropriations subcommittee, April 4, 2006 (https://www.c-span.org/supremeCourt/camerasInTheCourt/?justice=thomas) (last accessed December 19, 2022).

Index

Page references for figures are *italicized.*

ABC News, 23, 29, 70, 75, 78, 117n19,
    119n12
abortion, 28, 78–79, 85, 120n22
Affordable Care Act, 78–80
Alito, Samuel, 26, *54*, 55, 60
Al Odah v. United States, 10
American Bar Association, 3
amicus curiae briefs, 10–11, 30, 42, 66,
    123n15
Associated Press, 25, 50, 61, 89
*Atlantic Coast Pipeline, LLC v.
    Cowpasture River Assn.
    (Consolidated),* 24
attorneys, quoted in print media, 57–58,
    58, 60, 61

Baier, Bret, 76
*Barr, Atty Gen v. American Assn. of
    Political Consultants, Inc.,*
    37, 55
Barrett, Amy Coney, 26, *54,* 81–82,
    116n15, 122n4, 124n7
Baze v. Rees, 10
Bennett, W. Lance, 14, 34, 122n8
Bensen, Steve, 5
Biskupic, Joan, 116n15
Blackmun, Harry A., 11

Blatt, Lisa, 20, *20*
Boston Globe, 23, 61, 89, 119n12
Boumediene v. Bush, 10
Breyer, Stephen, 20, *20,* 26, *54,* 55,
    58
broadcast media:
    consumption of, 69
    data collection methodology, 26–29,
        29, 120n18
    dramatic unity technique, 76, 125n9
    effects of livestreaming oral
        arguments on, 3
    nature of coverage data, 75–82, *78*
    nature of coverage hypothesis, 15,
        70, 85–86, 89–90
    vs. print media, 75–76
    story content through word clouds,
        83–85, *83, 84, 85*
    volume of coverage data, 70–75, *71,
        72, 74*
    volume of coverage hypothesis,
        14–15, 69–70, 85–86, 89–90
Bush v. Gore, 9, 117n29

California v. Texas, 78–80
case salience, 30, 37, 39, 42, 73, 78–79,
    121n29

127

CBS News, 29, 70, 73, 75, 76, 117n19, 119n12
Chiafalo v. Washington, 37, 55, 56, 71, 80, 88, 124n8
Chicago Tribune, 119n12
Civil Liberties Cases, 30, 42, 66
Clark, Tom S., 30, 42, 121n29
CNN, 22, 23, 25, 26, 27–28, 29, 47–48, 50, 51, 70, 71–74, 78–82, 116n15, 117n19, 118n43, 119n12
Colorado Dept. of State v. Baca, 124n8
Constitutional Cases, 30, 42, 43, 66
Coons, Chris, 79–80
Court. *See* US Supreme Court
COVID-19 pandemic:
    effects of, 17–18, 69
    and oral argument protocols, 1–2, 8–9
C-SPAN, 20, *20*, 33, 122n4

Deferred Action for Childhood Arrivals (DACA) program, 74, 78
Department of Homeland Security v. Regents of Univ. of CA, 73, 74, 78, 83
Department of Homeland Security v. Thuraissigiam, 37
De Vogue, Ariane, 26
digital conferencing platforms, 17–18
Dobbs v. Jackson Women's Health Organization, 26, 37, 39, 55–56, 64, 73, 78–79, 85
Doocy, Peter, 76

Ex Parte Milligan, 119n5

FBI v. Fazaga, 64
federal holidays, 33, 121n2
Finn, Matt, 77
First Monday in October, 33–34, 44, 121n3, 122n4
Fox Business Network, 23, 25, 70, 119n12, 121n25
Fox News, 22, 23, 29, 70, 71–73, 75, 76–78, 81–82, 117n19, 119n12

Ginsburg, Ruth Bader, 26, *54*, 60, 124n7
Goodyear's India Rubber Glove Manufacturing Co. v. Goodyear Rubber Co., 48
Google Meet, 17
Google News, 33
Gorsuch, Neil, 26, *54*, 60
Grassley, Chuck, 3
Guardian, 87

Hamdi v. Rumsfeld, 9
Harlan, John M., 11
Heimerl, Florian, 126n18
Hitt, Matthew P., 6–7, 27
Honig, Elie, 81, 82
House, Toni, 7
Houston, Rachel, 33

institutional change, 4, 44–45, 90
institutions, defined, 4, 13

Jackson Women's Health Organization, 26
Johnson, Timothy R., 33
journalists:
    and justices, 116n15
    and "McNews" culture, 14, 118n41
Judicial Conference of the United States, 18
justices:
    and case salience measures, 30, 42
    and journalists, 116n15
    and public relations, 116n15
    quoted in print media, 52–57, *53*, *54*, *56*, 58–61, *60*, 65–67, *66*, *68*, 89
    uses of oral arguments by, 11–13
    video recording concerns of, 5, 16, 58, 61, 92, 124n5

Kagan, Elena, 12, 26, *54*, 55, 77
Katyal, Neal, 81
Kavanaugh, Brett, 26, *54*, 55, 60, 77, 122n4
Kelly v. United States, 24

Kennedy, Anthony, 11
Kennedy v. Bremerton School Dist., 39, 76

latent salience, 121n29
L.A. Times, 117n19
Lax, Jeffrey R., 121n29
Leahy, Patrick, 3
LexisNexis Academic (LNA), 27, 121n24
Liptak, Adam, 116n15
Little Sisters of the Poor Saints Peter and Paul Home v. Pennsylvania, 30, 37, 42, 55, 71, 80, 88
Livingston, Steven, 14, 34, 122n8
Los Angeles Times, 23, 30, 119n12

Martinez, Judy Perry, 3
McAdams, Katherine C., 22
McGirt v. Oklahoma, 37, 55
media. *See* broadcast media; news media; print media
Media Bias Chart, 23, 39, 120n14, 122n11, 123m12
Meredith, Mark, 77
methodology:
 broadcast news coverage data collection, 26–29, *29*, 120n18
 news outlet data collection, 21–23, *22*, *23*
 oral argument and case-level data collection, 30
 print news coverage data collection, 23–26, *25*, 120n13
Microsoft Teams, 17
MSNBC, 5, 25, 70, 71, 73–74, 79, 81–82, 119n12
Musberger, Robert B., 125n9

National Archives and Records Administration (NARA), 1, 9
National Public Radio, 116n15, 117n31
nature of media coverage. *See* online print media; broadcast media

NBC News, 70, 73–74, 117n19, 119n12
NCAA v. Alston, 76–77
Newsday, 25, 50, 61, 89, 119n12
news media:
 adaptation to changes in oral argument access, 13–15
 consumption of, 69
 data collection methodology, 21–23, *23*
 difficulty of covering SCOTUS, 6–7
 effects of livestreaming oral arguments on, 2–3, 21
 gatekeeping model of coverage, 14, 122n8
 ideological diversity of, 22–23, *23*
 influence on pubic support for SCOTUS, 4–5
 nature of coverage, 15, 118n42
 press passes, 19, 117n19, 119n12
 public reliance on, 5
 and public support for SCOTUS, 87–88
 twenty-four-hour news cycle, 6, 15, 117n18, 120n18
 volume of coverage, 14–15.
 See also broadcast media; print media
newswires, 124n11
New York Post, 22, 50, 61, 89, 119n12
New York State Rifle and Pistol Assn. v. Bruen, 64, 73, 80
New York Times, 25, 26–27, 30, 50, 51, 116n15, 117n19, 118n43, 119n12, 122n4
NFIB v. Sebelius, 10

Obergefell v. Hodges, 10
online print media:
 vs. broadcast media, 75–76
 cases garnering most coverage, 37–39, *38*
 coverage by ideology of outlet, 39–41, *40*
 data collection methodology, 23–26, *25*, 120n13

effects of livestreaming oral
arguments on, 2–3
inverted triangle of reporting, 125n9
nature of coverage data, 49–65, *51,
53, 54, 56, 57, 59, 60, 62, 63*
nature of coverage hypothesis, 15,
48–49, 67–68, 89
nature of coverage methods and
model, 65–67, *66, 68,* 124n10,
124n13
online vs. physical, 23–24
oral argument audio clip use, 62–65,
63
original reporting, livestreaming
effect on, 61–62, *62,* 124n6
quotation use, livestreaming effect
on, 52–61, *53, 54, 56, 57, 59, 60,*
89
story length, livestreaming effect on,
50–52, *51*
volume of coverage data, 35–41, *36,
38, 40*
volume of coverage hypothesis,
14–15, 34–35, 44–45, 88–89
volume of coverage methods and
model, 41–44, *43, 44,* 123n13,
123n16
oral arguments:
audio clip use in print media, 62–65,
63
audio recordings of, 1–2, 9
COVID-19 effects on, 1–2, 8–9
data collection methodology, 30
livestreaming of, 1–2, 49, 87–88, 90,
91, 116n11
in-person, 1, 115n1
public access to, 7–10, 13, 19–20
purposes of, 11–13
same day audio release of, 9–10,
117n31
scarcity of seating for, 2, 5, 6, 7, 19,
116n17, 119n10
transcript release of, 10
via telephonic audio conference, 18,
19

video coverage of, 91–93
Ortagus, Morgan, 77
*Our Lady of Guadalupe v. Morrissey-
Berru,* 39, 55

Palkot, Greg, 77
*Patent & Trademark Office v. Booking.
com,* 20, *20,* 33, 47–48, 55,
56, 62–63, 71–72, 80, 84, 88,
122n9
PBS, 29, 70, 71–73, 75, 81, 119n12
Pechman, Marsha J., 18
Pergram, Chad, 77
Pew Research Center, 17, 24
*Planned Parenthood of Southeastern
Pennsylvania v. Casey,* 7
Powell, Lewis F., 11
Pre-Argument Stories, 30, 43, 55–56,
66
Prelogar, Elizabeth, 26
public access:
to elected representatives, 7, 8–9,
117n27
to oral arguments, 7–10, 13, 19–20
to SCOTUS, 3–4, 90

quotation use in print media:
of attorneys, 57–58, *57, 60,* 61
of justices, 52–57, *53, 54, 56,* 58–61,
60, 65–67, *66, 68*
livestreaming effect on, 52, 89

Ramirez v. Collier, 64
Rehnquist, William H., 9
Rice, Douglas, 121n29
Rikelman, Julie, 26
Ritter, Matt, 6
Roberts, John, 1, 3, 9, 11–12, 25, 26,
47, *54,* 55, 58, 77, 87, 91
Roe v. Wade, 39, 120n22
Ross, Erica, 47–48
Rumsfeld v. Padilla, 10

*Sanchez v. Mayorkas, Sec. of Homeland
Security,* 58

Scalia, Antonin, 11
SCOTUS. *See* US Supreme Court
Searles, Kathleen, 6–7, 27
Senate Judiciary Committee, 3
Serrie, Jonathan, 76
Solicitor General's office, 15, 26, 30, 42, 66
Sotomayor, Sonia, 12, 26, *54*, 60, 77
Spanish flu pandemic (1918), 18, 115n2
Star Tribune (Minneapolis), 23, 119n12
Stegall, Casey, 76–79
Stewart, Scott, 26
Supreme Court Bar, 3
Supreme Court Judicial Data Base, 30

Talkin, Pamela, 64, 87
technology:
    digital conferencing platforms, 17–18, 119n3–4
    livestreaming, 13–15, 34–35
Thomas, Clarence, 26, 27–28, 47–48, 53, *54*, 60, 81–82, 92
Toobin, Jeffrey, 81–82
Totenberg, Nina, 116n15
Trump, Donald, 17, 80
Trump v. Hawaii, 10
Trump v. Mazars, 37, 39, 55, 64, 80, 83–84, 88, 124n8
Trump v. New York, 79, 82
Trump v. Vance, 30, 42, 71, 80, 84, 124n8

United States v. Sineneng-Smith, 24
United States v. Texas, 64, 73, 80, 85
USAID v. Alliance for Open Society International, Inc., 55
USA Today, 22, 87, 117n19, 118n43, 119n12

US Bureau of Labor Statistics, 69
US Forest Service v. Cowpasture River Assn., 24
US House of Representatives, 80, 117n27
US Senate, 117n27
US Supreme Court:
    blog of, 118n43
    COVID-19 response, 8–9
    difficulty of covering, 6–7
    news media reporting on, 1–3
    oral argument protocols, 1–2
    postponement of argruments, 18
    public access to, 3–4, 7–10, 90
    public support for, 4–5, 87–88
    rules of, 117n30
    sessons/sittings, 119n11
    terms, 33, 44, 115n6, 117n21
    transparancy in, 93–94
    video recording concerns of, 16, 58, 61, 92, 124n5

volume of media coverage. *See* online print media; broadcast media

Wall Street Journal, 25, 50, 117n19, 119n12
Washington Post, 3, 22, 25, 30, 50, 51, 58, 91, 117n19, 119n12
Whole Woman's Health v. Jackson, 64
Williams, Brian, 81
Williams, Pete, 82
word clouds, 83–85, *83*, *84*, *85*, 126n18

Yopp, Jan Johnson, 22

Zoom, 17

About the Authors

Rachael B. Houston is assistant professor of American judicial politics at Texas Christian University, where she studies judicial behavior, political communication, and social psychology. She is interested in how people learn, and form opinions, about the US Supreme Court, particularly with an emphasis on the role the media plays in informing the public. Her work has been published in *Justice System Journal, Journal of Supreme Court History*, and a variety of law journals, encyclopedias, and blogs.

Timothy R. Johnson is Horace T. Morse Distinguished Professor of Political Science and Law at the University of Minnesota. He has authored or coauthored three previous books about the Supreme Court including *Oral Arguments and Coalition Formation on the U.S. Supreme Court* (2012), *A Good Quarrel* (2009), and *Oral Arguments and Decision Making on the U.S. Supreme Court* (2001). He has also published more than forty articles and book chapters about the Court and the American judiciary. His commentary and research have been covered by *The Economist, The Guardian, The New York Times, The Washington Post, The Wall Street Journal, NPR, C-SPAN, Slate, USA Today, ABC, CNN,* and *WCCO*. Along with research, Johnson is passionate about teaching. Since 2006, he has mentored 14 graduate students and, since 2000, more than 200 undergraduate research projects. In 2018, he was named a semi-finalist for the prestigious Robert F. Cherry Award for Great Teaching (Baylor University) and was awarded the American Political Science Association's Distinguished Teaching Award.

Eve M. Ringsmuth is associate professor of political science at Oklahoma State University where she studies judicial politics, American political institutions, and civic education. Her coauthored book, *It's Not Personal: Politics* *and Policy in Lower Court Confirmation Hearings,* examines how senators use lower court confirmation hearings to advocate for preferred policies and increase their chance of re-election while also performing one of their core constitutional functions. Her research has been published in journals such as *American Politics Research, International Studies Quarterly, Political Behavior, Political Research Quarterly,* and *PS: Political Science & Politics.* Ringsmuth's research and commentary have been included in *The New York Times, The Washington Post, SCOTUSblog,* and *The Conversation.* She is also an enthusiastic teacher and, in 2020, received the Regents' Distinguished Teaching Award from Oklahoma State University.